IMANI RITUALS

NURTURING AFRICAN SPIRITUAL HERITAGE

Anthony Y. Stringer, PhD, Ayanna Kafi,
Duncan E. Teague, MDiv

 Published by Skinner House Books, an imprint of the Unitarian Universalist Association, 24 Farnsworth St., Boston, MA 02210–1409.

www.skinnerhouse.org

Printed in the United States

Cover design by Alex Camlin
Text design by Tim Holz

print ISBN: 978-1-55896-960-5
eBook ISBN: 978-1-55896-961-2

6 5 4 3 2 1
30 29 28 27 26 25

Library of Congress Cataloging-in-Publication Data

Names: Stringer, Anthony Y., author.
Title: Imani rituals : nurturing African spiritual heritage / Anthony Y. Stringer, PhD, Ayanna Kafi, Duncan E. Teague, MDiv.
Description: Boston, Massachusetts : Skinner House Books, [2025] | Summary: "Theologically inclusive and widely adaptable to liberal faith and humanist settings, Imani Rituals offers practices applicable to any context in which diversity and the inclusion of African Diasporan-inspired cultural practices are valued"-- Provided by publisher.
Identifiers: LCCN 2024041791 (print) | LCCN 2024041792 (ebook) | ISBN 9781558969605 (print) | ISBN 9781558969612 (ebook)
Subjects: LCSH: Religion and culture--Africa. | Religions--African influence. | African diaspora. | Unitarianism--United States.
Classification: LCC BL2400 .S776 2025 (print) | LCC BL2400 (ebook) | DDC 299.6/14--dc23/eng/20241025
LC record available at https://lccn.loc.gov/2024041791
LC ebook record available at https://lccn.loc.gov/2024041792

Contents

This book is dedicated to my ancestors: enslaved midwife and great-great-grandmother, Sylvia Jones (1810–?); formerly enslaved rape survivor, midwife, entrepreneur, philanthropist, and maternal great-grandmother, Francis Jones Wilson (1855–1942); child of Francis's rape whose white skin belied a fiercely Black identity, family matriarch, and maternal grandmother, Laura Jones Washington (1876–1969); railroad brakeman, minister, family patriarch, and grandfather, Joseph Washington (1872–1916); feminist and fiercely independent paternal grandmother, Lula Stringer (1866–1942); plumber, electrician, pioneering businessman, and father, Young Stringer (1907–1962); nurse, artist, and mother, Laura Washington Stringer (1912–2000); farmer, uncle, and father surrogate, Albert Washington (1898–1976); stillborn brother, whose name means "Do not forget me," Koofrey Henry (1950); and all those ancestors of African descent whose names have not been passed down to me.

—Dr. Anthony Y. Stringer

This book is for Mathew P. Taylor, Elandria Williams, and others from the Unitarian Universalist African Diaspora that we lost during the multiple pandemics.

—Ayanna Kafi

I dedicate my participation in this examination of rituals to Sister Kizzie Ricks and Mother Delsie Jackson, two senior African American women and church mothers at Westminster Baptist Church in Kansas City, Missouri. They saw my ministry as real and important long before I heard the call. I am grateful for the Westminster Church where my father, the now retired Rev. Russell L. Teague, pastored with the dedication and support of my late mother Alyce Jean Teague. My childhood spiritual home was the foundation for who I became as I grew up and embraced Unitarian Universalism. Finally, I am grateful for Dr. Anthony and Ayanna Kafi Stringer's invitation to contribute to this book.

—Rev. Duncan E. Teague

Broadening the Rituals of Unitarian Universalism and Other Liberal Faiths

Is there a place for ritual in Unitarian Universalism? The answer to this question has varied over time. As a creedless faith, Unitarian Universalism eschews dogma and embraces reason and tolerance of varying beliefs and customs. A faith that can broadly encompass theistic and humanist themes faces a challenge in finding religious customs and rituals that satisfy diverse spiritual cravings. In earlier decades, one solution was to avoid rituals as much as possible. Indeed, one of the authors remembers his first time visiting a UU congregation and being surprised to hear two members complaining to each other about the minister's effrontery in lighting a candle during worship. Three decades later, this same congregation now incorporates everything from chalice and candle lighting to liturgical dance to create an often theatrical worship experience. Nonetheless, when ritual elements are included in UU worship and congregational life, they typically are drawn from European American cultures and traditions.

Consequently, a better question to ask today is whether there is a place for a broader ritual cloth that captures the diverse cultures and heritages of the people who seek a home within contemporary liberal faiths. By *ritual*, we are not referring to mere habit, the routines each of us performs on a recurring basis. We are not referring to that morning cup of coffee while reading the newspaper, the evening stroll through the park with a canine companion, or the nightly dive into a YouTube or Facebook rabbit hole. We are also not referring to the casual and often perfunctory habits we adopt as part of our religious gatherings—the obligatory ways we start our meetings with a candle or chalice lighting, a one-word check-in to express how we're feeling, a familiar and well-worn prayer or reading that we partly listen to while simultaneously enumerating the tasks we failed to complete today. Instead, when we are speaking of ritual, we are speaking of something far deeper and far more engaging.

We have all had moments when feelings welled up, spilled over, and overwhelmed us. That awestruck gasp at the endless night sky, that unspeakable tenderness inspired by a lover's gaze, that celebratory joy when friends reunite after forced separation, that passion and purpose when a community stands together for what it knows is just and right. These are the very feelings ritual is meant to inspire. Expanding our original question, we consider, is there room in liberal religious life for this type of ritual that draws upon wellsprings of human emotion? Do religious traditions that wed themselves to human reason risk divorcing themselves from human passion?

The context in which we ask these questions is one of growing diversity within UU and other liberal Protestant faiths, and specifically the growing appeal these faiths have for African Americans. The Pew Research Center survey of 8,660 Black Americans between 2019 and 2020 shows that while a majority who participate in services attend predominantly Black congregations, a third do not.[1] Of those who are looking for new churches, 63 percent do not place great importance on whether members share their same racial background. In this context, the questions we ask can be further refined to explore

1 Besheer Mohamed et al., *Faith Among Black Americans*, Pew Research Center, February 16, 2021, https://www.pewresearch.org/religion/2021/02/16/faith-among-black-americans/.

how well liberal religious churches can meet the spiritual needs and ritual expectations of African Americans who seek them out.

Some sense of how equipped these liberal congregations are to meet the needs of African Americans may be found in contrasting the experiences of respondents to the Pew Survey who attend predominantly Black churches with those attending congregations that are predominantly White. Spontaneous physical (including dancing and jumping) and vocal (shouting or saying "amen") expressions during worship occur in 76 percent and 99 percent, respectively, of Black Protestant churches, but in only 37 percent and 81 percent of White or White-led churches that African Americans attend. Contrasts appear even in private rituals. Seventy-nine percent of Black Americans pray daily while only 44 percent of liberal White Protestants do.[2] A third of Black Americans pray to their ancestors, an option so unlikely to be endorsed by White Protestants that surveys do not ask them.

We believe there is room for rich and emotionally engaging ritual in liberal religion generally, and specifically in the UU faith tradition. The cultural and spiritual tapestry of the African Diaspora can be a source of profoundly moving and satisfying ritual, not only for African Americans but for all those who seek out and thrive within liberal religious communities. Little evidence, however, is to be found of this rich tapestry being utilized.

A search of the Unitarian Universalist Association website provides compelling proof that UUs yearn for ritual and have created dozens of rituals in response to this yearning.[3] Many of the rituals

2 Gregory A. Smith, *About Three-in-Ten U.S. Adults Are Now Religiously Unaffiliated*, Pew Research Center, December 14, 2021, https://www.pewresearch.org/religion/2021/12/14/about-three-in-ten-u-s-adults-are-now-religiously-unaffiliated/.

3 "Rituals for Worship," Unitarian Universalist Association, https://www.uua.org/worship/words/ritual.

center on life transitions, including child dedications and baptisms, youth-bridging ceremonies, marriages and civil unions, and memorial services. Another large group of rituals center on lay and professional religious life. This includes new member ceremonies, religious educator commissions, and ministerial ordinations and installations. Unitarian Universalists create rituals in response to urgent contemporary concerns—a fire and water ritual in response to wildfires in Australia, a cider and cornbread ritual in response to Syrian and other refugee crises, a candle lighting ritual in response to the Covid pandemic.

With few exceptions, most UU rituals are monocultural, which is to say, they reflect White, European-origin culture. Even when UU rituals are international in scope, as in an ingathering water ceremony that connects us to places around the world or a water communion that mentions the multiple religious traditions that inspire our faith—from Christianity to Taoism—our rituals are still primarily verbal and reflective in nature. They make you think. They don't necessarily make you feel.

The most emotionally engaging of the rituals are those that spring from a diverse cultural well. Among these are a pagan ritual of cleansing that involves multiple senses through acts of washing and anointing, a Christian-inspired ritual that gives thanks through the sharing of freshly baked bread, a Jewish-inspired ritual that includes the blowing of the shofar, a New Orleans jazz funeral for the passing of a year that is centered in Black and Creole tradition, and a blessing of the entry into womanhood based in the Hispanic tradition of quinceañera. Such rituals are alive with tradition and heritage. They don't just make you reflect. They stir your spirit and get you moving in whatever ways your body allows. They remind you of ancient ways and times while providing a contemporary meaning and context that allows you to tread down well-worn spiritual paths while wearing comfortably new soles (read *souls*).

Why then does Unitarian Universalism, a religion that claims six sources encapsulating much of the human theological heritage, not have a broader body of ritual to draw upon? Why is the tapestry of our faith woven in monochromatic threads?

There is good reason for our reticence to broaden the ritual tapestry. We worry about cultural appropriation—in other words, the exploitation of another culture, particularly one that has been minoritized, marginalized, and oppressed by "us."[4] The issue, however, is complicated. The "us" refers to the dominant culture, which within Unitarian Universalism and other liberal faiths tracing their origins to the Protestant Reformation is White and European. As the collective "we" expands to include more diverse people, we are forced to rethink what we mean by "us." Among the authors of this book, one of us was raised as a UU (Ayanna), another was raised in his father's Black Christian church (Duncan), and a third spent his adolescence in a church that centered equally activism and Afrocentrism (Tony). Yet each of us individually has spent over three decades as committed UUs. Our collective "we" is not encapsulated within the typical "us." If avoidance of cultural appropriation means we do not embrace the culture and traditions of Africa and the African Diaspora, then it means we too are outside the UU embrace.

We want to bring our culture with us. We want to experience Unitarian Universalism in a context that is familiar to the senses. We want the sights, sounds, tastes, smells, and emotions that are our heritage. We want the same freedom that UUs who come from Christian, Jewish, and other cultural and spiritual backgrounds have to derive practices from their heritage in shaping their UU faith. Many UU Christians celebrate Easter differently than they did before they

4 Ijeoma Oluo, "What is cultural appropriation?," in *So You Want to Talk About Race* (Seal Press, 2018).

became UU. The same can be said for the way UUs of Jewish ancestry and heritage engage with the High Holy Days within their current UU congregations. Arguably, African American UUs desire even more the freedom to create new ritual and tradition within the framework of our heritage, given that ours is a culture known for syncretism and improvisation. We riff culturally because riffing is part of who we are.

This brings us to another complicated question. How far back should the reworking of African American ritual go? We are part of the African Diaspora, but we are not African. When we wear kente cloth graduation stoles, display Adinkra symbols on our walls, pour libations to our ancestors, and give our children African names, we are honoring cultural traditions that are newly discovered rather than directly handed down, as we attempt to link ourselves to a past that enslavement did its best to obliterate.

We have each been to one or more African countries: one of us as a visitor (Ayanna) and two of us (Tony and Duncan) as part of their professional work. In an extended stay in Rwanda, Tony realized that the same word, *mzungu*, used to describe his White colleagues was used to describe him as well. It did not refer to skin color; it referred to being someone who had wandered from their home. In one particularly moving encounter, Tony listened to a Rwandan artist and genocide survivor's story. In turn, Tony shared the story of his great-grandmother's rape at the hands of a White man not long after being emancipated from enslavement in America. Much to Tony's surprise, the remote suffering of his great-grandmother brought tears to the artist's eyes, despite his much more immediate and personal experience of genocidal violence. It also ended the artist's use of *mzungu* for Tony, as he recognized the harm it did to so directly link one whose ancestral home was lost to those who had taken him from it.

Though we are not African, we are also not *mzungu*. Heredity links us to Africa, but even more importantly, a shared heritage of pain links us to this distant homeland. The conversation around cultural appropriation must acknowledge the difference between someone who is White and European American and someone who is Black and African American finding a source for faith and ritual in the spiritual traditions of Africa and the African Diaspora. Even in the latter case, when an African American lays claim to their full spiritual and cultural heritage from Africa and beyond, care must be taken to credit the source and to not profit by claiming to be something we are not or doing something we cannot. In writing this book, we are not trying to profit from imitating what is not ours.

For example, the Discernment/Divination ritual in this book pays homage to the intricate divination systems of the Yoruba, Ibo, Fulani, and other peoples, without attempting to imitate or replicate them. Instead, these traditions inspire a birthday ritual that encourages friends and family to bring the gift of "divination" through thoughtful and caring advice. All rituals acknowledge the traditions that inspire them without imitating or copying them. Although some rituals recommend ministers lead parts of ceremonies, anyone can take on the role of ritual leader. The materials, setting, preparation, language, and practices required are fully described so that in most cases the rituals can be performed by laity or clergy. The verbal parts of each ritual appear in a different font to make it easy to tell the script from the directions. By making the rituals available and replicable, we seek to avoid any opportunity for exploitation and profit.

There is still more complexity, however, for us to interrogate. When we say that a ritual is inspired by an African tradition, we are admitting to riffing off the original, to not faithfully following tradition. UUs do this all the time, but is it right to do so? On the flip side, what are the consequences of not doing so?

We believe there is great wisdom and knowledge, as well as passion and beauty, in the multitude of ways human beings have invented to evoke the sacred. Indeed, part of what drew all three of us to Unitarian

Universalism were the six sources and the opportunity they afforded for unfettered embrace of universal wisdom, beauty, knowledge, and passion. To fail in that embrace deprives us of large parts of the human spiritual tradition that are salvific. To fail to embrace the traditions of Africa is to continue the historic and systemic devaluation of people of color and all that we create.

Some traditions, however, will not enter the modern world unchanged. Marriages between elderly men and young children are not acceptable in most parts of the world, for example. This is the case for many rituals and traditions that have their origins in the cultures of Africa and its diaspora. The traditions will enter contemporary practice only when changed for a contemporary context. Such traditions will be lost to human posterity if they are not capable of evolution and adaptation to current circumstances.

Despite a history that stretches back centuries, Unitarian Universalism is forever evolving and consequently is always contemporary. In broadening the fabric of UU ritual to encompass the traditions of people of color, what we introduce will necessarily reflect present societal contexts and circumstances.

Imani is Kiswahili for faith.[5] The eighteen imani rituals in this book are intended for individual, family, congregational, and community

5 The Arabic language also has the word *imani* (sometimes spelled "amani") with the similar meaning of "faithful." The word *imani* may have entered Swahili from Arabic given the proximity of Arabic and Swahili speaking peoples. However, it more likely entered Swahili from the Hausa language, which is spoken in several countries in west and central Africa where Swahili is also spoken. Hausa and Arabic languages share many words, and some linguists believe they are cognate languages, both descended from an earlier common language that has gone extinct. Regardless of the language in which it originated, the word *imani* has a secular meaning in Arabic, Hausa, and Swahili and is not exclusively associated with any religion, including Islam. It likely existed as a secular word even among Arabic speakers before the Islamic religion appeared.

practice. The individual rituals include meditations to promote a sense of spiritual possession, transcendence, and acceptance of change. The family rituals focus on, among other topics, remembering ancestors and honoring elders. Congregational and community rituals include prayer, feasting, and celebrations of freedom and Kwanzaa. In many instances, the language of the rituals can be modified for different settings so that each can be flexibly adapted to meet multiple needs. Options for varying each ritual are included, but even these should be considered points of departure that may stimulate the reader's own ideas for ritual variations. The rituals are intended to address real human needs in ways that are meaningful, emotionally engaging, and culturally inclusive.

While the rituals in this book are written from a Unitarian Universalist perspective, none of the rituals is exclusively the province of UUs. They are theologically inclusive and widely adaptable to liberal faith and humanist settings. Many of the rituals are appropriate for family and secular community contexts. Hence, *Imani Rituals* is applicable to any context in which diversity and the inclusion of African Diasporan-inspired cultural practices are valued.

This leads us to our final set of questions. How inclusive are the rituals intended to be? Are they only intended for use by African Americans? Can White people participate without it becoming an instance of cultural appropriation? The answer is again more complicated than simply yes or no. For example, the Karamu ritual celebrates African American heritage and unity. It uses a table divided into color-coded sections representing different times in the African American experience in the United States. The ritual includes the words: *Let us gather around our communal table. Each area symbolizes an era of African American history. The black area of our table reminds us of our time before slavery when we lived in peace and freedom in Africa. I pour a libation to our African Ancestors, known and unknown, from that era.* These words would obviously ring hollow if not spoken by an African American. People of other ethnicities and backgrounds can be welcome guests at the table, bringing food with them to the feast, but the ritual is for African Americans.

Contrastingly, prayer, spiritual transcendence, ancestorship, ancestor remembrance, and other rituals do not include language or practices that are appropriate only for people of color. While inspired by African and African Diasporan cultures, they are universal rituals. UUs seek the universal within the particular. There are universals within the particularities of African-inspired spirituality. It is those universals that are Africa's contribution to the canon of human spirituality and which are, through these rituals, our contributions to Unitarian Universalism and other liberal faiths. If permission is needed, then permission is given to practice what is universal within our heritage. To do so honors that heritage and affirms that Unitarian Universalism values it as part of the "Earth-centered traditions which celebrate the sacred circle of life and instruct us to live in harmony with the rhythms of nature." The earth includes Africa, its offspring living around the world, and the traditions they bring or create. If we fail to broaden the tapestry of UU faith to include the vitality of Africa's descendants, then Unitarian Universalism will be poorer for it.

We close this introduction with a quote from Pope John Paul II during his visit to Ghana in 1980:

> Africa has something distinctive to offer to the world. . . . A vision of the world where the sacred is central; a deep awareness of the link between Creator and nature; a great respect for all life; a sense of family and of community that blossoms into an open and joyful hospitality; reverence for dialogue as a means of settling differences and sharing insights; spontaneity and the joy of living expressed in

> poetic language, song and dance. All these aspects manifest a culture with an all-encompassing spiritual dimension. This is what makes the African culture unique. . . .
>
> Each nation brings to the family of nations its own cultural contribution, and through the legitimate expression of values and traditions there is possible a harmony among peoples that transcends partisan differences, prejudices and rivalries. Such a harmony, built on respect for and openness towards the values of others, in particular their moral and spiritual values, facilitates the possibility of concerted action on problems that extend beyond the borders of individual nations. Africa is called to bring fresh ideals and insights to a world that shows signs of fatigue and selfishness.[6]

We hope to fulfill this prophetic vision, at least in some small measure, through the rituals that follow.

6 Pope John Paul II, "Meeting of John Paul II with the President of Ghana" (speech, Apostolic Pilgrimage to Africa, Accra, Ghana, May 8, 1980), https://www.vatican.va/content/john-paul-ii/en/speeches/1980/may/documents/hf_jp-ii_spe_19800508_president-ghana.html.

Making Rituals Universally Accessible

The authors wish to thank Mary Beth Spencer for her accessibility review of this book and for the initial draft of this section on principles of Universal Access design.

Universal Access is an approach to design in which the goal is to be inclusive of people with differing abilities from the beginning, rather than later making exceptions to include individuals who have disabilities or functional needs. This isn't always the easiest approach to design, but it is the most welcoming. While the principle of universal access should guide ritual design, how close you come to achieving it will depend upon the ritual, your group, your setting, and other factors known only to you. While it is impossible to create an exhaustive list of things to do for every ritual to achieve universal access, the following ideas will help guide you in making your rituals as accessible as possible for your unique situation. Making one improvement each time, including small improvements that accumulate over time, can result in rituals that are accessible and inviting.

Setting

Make sure the building is open and welcoming to all. Use buildings with fewer steps and stairs and with accessible restrooms. Ensure there is enough room for everyone. If participants will be in a circle, make sure it is wide enough for all, with spaces for participants in wheelchairs to enter and join. Make sure this is true even if the circle is expanded. If people are viewing a low table, ensure that those who cannot stand are in the front. If participants are seated in a congregation setting, ensure there are cutouts for wheelchair users throughout so those with disabilities can choose where to sit. If you are creating a specific sacred space, such as a circle, explain how people should enter and exit the circle and where to go to deal with bodily needs, such as restrooms and water.

Movement

If there will be movement as part of the ritual, ensure that you explicitly mention a plan for those who are not comfortable moving. Some suggestions might be having volunteers bring materials to them, asking a beloved to stand in their stead, asking the person leading the ritual to come to them, or having preferential seating. All of these could enable participation without excessive movement. Also, make sure there is enough space for everyone, including those in wheelchairs, to maneuver through the space safely.

Sound

Make sure that everyone can hear what you say adequately. Small groups of four to six may need no amplification. However, groups larger than that, particularly those with unknown participants, should be amplified whenever possible. It is often difficult for people to hear speakers, especially those who speak quietly. Small, easily transported sound systems can often be used for groups in settings where there is no permanent system. You may want to consider if it is possible to have your ritual closed-captioned in real time or to have sign language interpreters for those who need them. In any case, preferential seating for those who are hard of hearing or who are D/deaf is recommended.

Sight

Make sure participants with blindness or low vision are included by describing what everything looks like and what each person is doing. Remember that a period of silence does not have the same effect for someone who can't see what is happening. In using descriptive language, be sure to include all senses. Remove potential barriers and impediments to movement through the area. Eliminate unnecessarily winding or complicated paths. Offer to guide participants with low vision if they wish, and allow them to move at their own pace.

Cognitive Needs

Numerous medical conditions and medical treatments, including those that do not directly involve the brain, can alter or impair cognition. People may experience temporary or lasting "brain fog" as they undergo chemotherapy, convalesce after surgery, or recover from systemic infections. The likelihood of mild cognitive impairment disability or dementia increases with age. Even in the absence of illness, cognitive ability varies over the course of a lifetime. The effects are often on attention, memory, and thinking skills. Provide attention or fatigue breaks in long rituals. Have written, verbal, or other cues to remind participants of words to be spoken or actions to be performed. Vary the complexity of participant parts in the ritual according to individual comfort, allowing different cognitive entry points to participation. Cognition also can vary over the course of a day, with some individuals experiencing a decrease in their functioning in the evening. Participants who experience this may prefer rituals scheduled in the morning or midday, rather than in the evening. Cognition can also fluctuate over days and weeks, with people having transient variability in their functioning. Flexibility in scheduling rituals, including a willingness to reschedule, may help to accommodate these individuals especially when the ritual centers upon their participation.

Neurodivergence

If your ritual is long or energetic, requiring a lot of physical or emotional energy from participants, make sure there is a quiet place where they can go to relax and take a break from the activity and the stimulation. The goal is to decrease visual, auditory, and other sensory stimulation. This place may be in a separate room or in the same room but removed from the group. It should be comfortable and relaxing, allowing participants to calm down and recenter themselves before rejoining the group. Additionally, attendees may not like being touched by strangers. Provision should be made for participants to safely communicate their level of comfort with touch or physical proximity. An option to consider are colored wristbands that indicate preferences.

Scents

Many people are allergic or sensitive to scents and chemicals in the air. Ensure that your space is adequately ventilated if you are burning or spraying any scent, lotion, or chemical (natural or artificial) into the air. Whenever possible, it is better to use scent-free candles and other supplies. If you will be using scents or incense, let participants know so that they can take their own steps to protect themselves as necessary.

Other Disabilities

Consider other things you know about your group. Participants on crutches may need assistance carrying materials. Someone using oxygen may prefer to stay in one place. People undergoing, or who have recently undergone, medical procedures should be asked if they have functional needs. Some disabilities may not be apparent, and participants' preferences regarding how they are accommodated should not be assumed. Always inquire, allow individual preference to guide accommodations, and encourage people to make known their needs according to their comfort level.

THE IMANI RITUALS

Ancestor Remembrance

Purpose

To honor ancestors and other deceased individuals by remembering and sharing their lives and passing those memories to the next generation.

Historical Inspiration

Elmina Castle in Ghana was built by the Portuguese in 1492 as a trading post, a place of commerce where Europeans could barter with Africans. But once the fever for human commerce took hold in Europe and the Americas, Elmina Castle mutated into a place of cruelty and terror. Its storage rooms became dungeons, each packed with upwards of 300 African slaves in quarters so close that not even an arm could be raised. There they waited, shackled in darkness made fetid with human waste and sickness. There they waited as the mighty sound of the nearby Atlantic Ocean drowned out the continuous moans of misery and death.

Today Elmina Castle is a museum and a memorial of the Atlantic Slave Trade, one of the greatest tragedies of human history. A plaque at Elmina Castle now reads "In everlasting memory of the anguish of our ancestors." Living descendants have a duty to their ancestors. It is the duty to remember. A core belief in many parts of Africa is that a part of the ancestor survives while someone is alive who remembers.[7]

7 John S. Mbiti, *African Religions and Philosophy* (Anchor Books, 1970).

Occasion and Frequency

We suggest families practice this ritual annually on, or near, what was the birthday of the ancestor, deceased relative, chosen family, or cherished friend. A congregation may want to set aside a part of each worship service, a day each month, or a special annual holiday (e.g., Memorial Day) to remember ancestors.

Setting

This ritual may be held at home or at congregational or community venues.

Materials and Ritual Preparation

Create an altar to the deceased that includes photographs, belongings that have been handed down and kept, and other mementos of the person's life. Place a candle on the altar, a goblet filled with wine or juice, a small cup for each family member, and a bowl into which libations can be poured. Dim lighting, soft background music or chanting, and incense may be used to cultivate a meditative or reflective mood.

The Ritual (Family Version)

The oldest relative present who remembers the ancestor (whether directly or through stories), is most closely related, and who is able serves as the ritual leader. The leader begins by lighting the candle.

> We gather at this altar to honor and preserve the memory of my [state the familial relationship and name of the person to be remembered]. Here is how I remember [relationship and name].

The leader briefly narrates the person's life, including birth, death, and other important dates. The narration should include significant events, accomplishments, and anecdotes from the person's life. The objects placed on the table can be used to illustrate the narrative. The leader ends with:

> And that's how I remember [relationship and name]. I invite anyone else to speak who has memories of our ancestor to share.

After each person has spoken, the leader continues.

> Our ancestors believed that in death our bodies perish but that
> some part of us survives if someone is alive who remembers.
> Our ancestors' sacrifices and labors made our lives possible.
> We must honor them by remembering.

The leader pours a libation into the bowl and then raises the goblet for everyone to see.

> I honor the memory of [relationship and name].

The leader pours some wine from the goblet into their cup, drinks, and then passes the goblet on to the next oldest family member with the closest relationship to the ancestor. If an even older or closer relative was unable to serve as leader, this person should be next in line to receive the goblet.

Each person pours a libation, holds the goblet up, repeats the phrase used by the leader *("I honor the memory of . . .")*, and pours and takes a sip from their cup. This continues in order of age and familial relationship until each family member has had a turn. Each may share a personal anecdote about the ancestor before pouring their libation.

The leader then invites guests or friends present to pour a libation from the goblet into the bowl to honor the memory of the ancestor.

> I now invite any friend present to come, take the goblet, and to pour a libation. As you do, please say the words: I honor the memory of [name of ancestor].

Friends and guests should not drink the wine. This is reserved for family. The goblet may be refilled as needed. Friends may share a personal anecdote about the ancestor before pouring their libation.

The leader continues after all libations have been poured.

> Please join hands and repeat after me. Pause for repetition after each line break.

> May we each and all
> leave good memories
> for those who follow
> to honor us.

The leader signals the end of the ritual by extinguishing the candle and saying:

> Ashé.

Variations

We encourage adaptation of the basic ritual to unique needs and circumstances. Some families may want to drink directly from the goblet instead of using individual cups. Congregations may create altars that include representations of ancestors from many families, as well as public figures that are important to us all. In these instances, a minister may serve as ritual leader, or congregants representing each family may alternate in leading the ceremony. It is especially important to remember those who have lost their lives tragically to the violence of white supremacy and racism.

As part of a Memorial Day observance, a congregation may wish to commemorate local, national, or international events resulting in senseless loss of life, the remembrance of which is part of a commitment to never let such tragedies repeat. In these circumstances, individual names are sometimes lost or are too numerous to be recounted and the ritual leader may instead offer a more general remembrance. For example,

> I honor the memory of all the Black American soldiers who have fought for freedom on foreign shores only to return to a homeland that still refused to recognize their rights and humanity.

Questions for Discussion

- What qualifies one to be honored as an ancestor?
- Do a person's good deeds or the depth and breadth of their love matter more in gaining the status of ancestorship?
- No human being is perfect. What role does forgiveness play in conferring ancestorship?
- How do we balance honoring those who have departed with expressing our love, admiration, and thanks while people are still alive?
- How does a ritual such as this fit with your beliefs about whether there is life after death?

Ancestorship

Purpose

This ritual remembers and venerates ancestors and those now living who are on the verge of transitioning to ancestorship. The ritual allows the living to draw inspiration from the lives and legacies of ancestors and those nearing this final transition.

Historical Inspiration

Most societies erect monuments and create holidays to venerate great people of history. On a smaller scale, families everywhere preserve the memory of deceased relatives. In traditional African and African Diasporan communities, ancestor veneration is a particularly strong cultural characteristic. Libations are poured to honor and remember ancestors. Food is placed out for the ancestors to consume. Animals are sacrificed to bring the ancestors' good favor. Misfortune may be attributed to the anger of ancestors over a family's failure to honor them or failure to follow tradition. The ancestors' guidance and protection may be sought in desperate times.

Dying is necessary, but insufficient, to become an ancestor. Ancestorship is the culmination of a good life and is a status conferred upon the departed in proportion to their good works while living. Ancestorship is the reward for a life spent in service to family and community.[8]

8 Anthony Ephirim-Donkor, *African Spirituality: On Becoming Ancestors* (African World Press, 1998).

Unitarian Universalism similarly emphasizes good works done in one's lifetime as the hallmark of a good life.

Occasion and Frequency

Thoughts turn to ancestorship toward the end of life. Death, however, can come suddenly and unexpectedly. The subject is often difficult to talk about, even with elderly relatives. We often prefer to deny the inevitable rather than to face and prepare for it. There is no perfect time for this ritual, but there is plenty of time for regret if a loved one dies without their life story captured for remembrance and without them knowing how they will be remembered and revered.

Setting

This ritual is appropriate for home gatherings, including family meals. It may be included in the program of activities for a family reunion. It is also appropriate for smaller, one-on-one meetings with family members.

Materials

The ritual requires a means of recording the stories of aging family members. A written record or digital recording may be used. In choosing a recording method, consider that after the person's death, many family members may wish to receive a copy.

Ritual Preparation

Referring to the person's future death as a transition to ancestorship, or as "becoming an ancestor," may make discussion easier and lessen discomfort and denial over what is a natural part of everyone's life. Arrangements must be made for the family gathering, whether it is a small and intimate family meal or an extended family reunion.

Arrangements for the recording should also be made. One family member should serve as facilitator of the discussion. The person being honored with ancestorship should prepare to tell the story of their life. The facilitator can help by posing key questions that will elicit information family will want to know and keeping the story at the right length to hold everyone's attention. Family members who are particularly close to the person being honored should prepare a brief testimonial about what their relative means to them and how they will honor and remember them when they become an ancestor. The person being honored, and family members, can bring photos and other memorabilia to share during the ritual.

The Ritual (Family Version)

Facilitator: We have come together as a family to hear [Name]'s life story so that we may remember it, be inspired by it, and pass it on to all generations of our family. [Name], we love you, and we are here to listen to the story you have lived.

The facilitator can ask key questions here to help in telling the person's story. Other family members can ask questions about events they too wish to learn more about. Family photos and other material can be included.

Continue after the person's story has been told and recorded.

Many of us wish to say what you and your life mean to us and how we will honor and remember you as our ancestor.

Call on each person who wishes to share. The facilitator can also be among the sharers. Each person shares personally what the person has meant to them and the inspiration and wisdom they draw from the person, using any anecdotes or memorabilia that will tell their story. Each person ends with the concluding statement:

Sharers: You will be my ancestor and I will tell your story to all generations of our family who will honor and remember you just as I do.

Facilitator: Ancestorship is an honor that is achieved through a life that is full of love and service to others. Your life inspires, enriches, and sustains us all. We honor you with the gift of remembrance and ancestorship. Will you accept this honor so that your spirit may bless us and all future generations of our family?

The person being honored gives their acceptance and the family celebration begins.

Variations

Some may want to connect the ancestorship ritual with creating a will and durable power of attorney and sharing wishes for end-of-life care. It may also be an opportunity to share thoughts regarding a future memorial service.

If a person's death precedes the ritual, a family may gather to share stories about the person's life. Each relative ends with the statement:

[Name] will be my ancestor and I will tell their story to all generations of our family who will honor and remember them just as I do.

The facilitator can conclude with:

Ancestorship is an honor that is achieved through a life that is full of love and service to others. [Name]'s life inspires, enriches, and sustains us all. We honor [Name] with the gift of remembrance

> and ancestorship. May they accept this honor so that their spirit may bless us and all future generations of our family.

A similar situation occurs when an infant or child dies. In traditional societies, they would not be eligible for ancestor status. UU families, however, may wish to extend such an honor to even a short life. We find inspiration even in the youngest life and honor even the shortest existence with remembrance. While this is a departure from African source traditions, it accommodates contemporary needs and sensibilities. For example, Tony annually honors and remembers his mother's first child who did not survive childbirth. Doing so reminds him to hold compassion and care in his heart for the most vulnerable among us. Even a short life has much to teach us and is deserving of recognition through ancestorship.

Questions for Discussion

Facilitators of this ritual may find these or similar prompts helpful in structuring life stories: Tell us how your parents met and how you were born. Tell us about your favorite memories from childhood and adolescence. Tell us about your work. Tell us about your marriage.

- What are the happiest memories you have?
- What were the most difficult times in your life?
- What are you proudest of in your life?
- What do you see as the legacy of your life and work?
- What wisdom do you want to share with us?

Atonement and Forgiveness

Purpose

Release of guilt and regret while embracing forgiveness of self and others.

Historical Inspiration

African and African Diaspora spiritual traditions find within the material world a natural spirit that is beneficent despite the pain, misfortune, and cruelty that have long been a part of the African experience.[9] The fact that African spirituality manages to hold firm to a belief in a moral and beneficent universe, despite the direct and intense suffering of so many generations of Africans throughout the world, powerfully attests to the strength and durability of this spiritual tradition.

Morality within African spirituality is centered upon harmony. What is good and just is what promotes harmony with nature, within oneself, and within human communities.[10] When harmony is lacking, evil and human suffering emerge.

Harmony is often fleeting because conflict is built into the fabric of existence. Nature is full of dynamic and conflicting forces. The

9 Cosmas Okechukwu Obiego, *African Image of the Ultimate Reality* (Peter Lang, 1984).

10 Godwin Sogolo, *Foundations of African Philosophy: A Definitive Analysis of Conceptual Issues in African Thought* (Ibadan University Press, 1994).

same is true for our own inner lives. We have conflicting impulses with which we must constantly contend. The individual members of a community are often in conflict with one another as well, simply by virtue of their proximity. Communities are imperfect. Injustice can be woven into the character of a community, so that the community itself becomes a source of conflict and disharmony.

Ultimately, what restores harmony is love. Without harmony, all things are like loose and unconnected threads. Love weaves those threads together into that "single garment of destiny" that Martin Luther King Jr. spoke of so eloquently.[11] In contemporary interpretation, atonement is a loving act of restoration, not to appease an external deity but to end suffering and to absolve us of the guilt and shame we feel when our actions isolate and separate us from the larger order.

African Diasporic spirituality is simultaneously pessimistic and optimistic. While acknowledging suffering as an inevitable consequence of the existence of opposing forces and impulses, it never loses faith in the ultimate goodness of the universe, never loses hope for a restoration of harmony through atonement and forgiveness, and never ceases to believe in the possibility of change.[12] Unitarian Universalism is consistently optimistic about the possibilities for human growth and improvement and can easily accommodate the optimism in African spirituality. For UUs, the more pessimistic elements of African spirituality may serve as a healthy dose of realism about the nature of human existence.

11 Martin Luther King Jr., "Letter from Birmingham City Jail" (April 16, 1963).

12 Mary Cuthrell-Curry, "African-derived Religion in the African-American Community in the United States," in *African Spirituality: Forms, Meanings and Expressions*, ed. Jacob K. Olupona (Crossroad Publishing, 2000).

In contrast to the Christian doctrine of original sin, Unitarian Universalism affirms the inherent worth and dignity of human beings. UU optimism about humankind, however, leaves a void when it comes to addressing the reality of moral transgression and ethical compromise. Human beings are capable of both good and evil. If we acknowledge only the former, where is the sinner's path to atonement and forgiveness? The intent of this ritual is to provide such a path.

Occasion and Frequency

The ritual may be performed at any time in response to feelings of guilt, regret, or disconnection from self, community, or nature.

Setting and Materials

Perform the ritual in a circular space, either indoors or outdoors. Circular spaces are continuous, having no clear beginning or ending. The ritual space therefore reinforces a sense of continuity and connection. The size of this area will vary with the number of participants in the ritual and should be large enough to accommodate the ritual leader and several participants at a time. The sacred area is set apart by a symbolic border made of natural materials such as stones, flowers or flower petals, wood chips, shells, or leaves. The border only serves to demarcate the sacred space and does not need to be elaborate. One or more breaks in the border will serve as entry points to the sacred space.

If desired, a "guardian figure" can be placed at each entry point. The guardian figure symbolically reminds us that no thought or emotion (such as hate, jealousy, or greed) that separates one from another should be brought into the sacred space. Guardians may be as elaborate as a traditional African wood carved sculpture or as simple as a photo of an ancestor. If a more natural and symbolic guardian is desired, a tower constructed of rocks may serve the purpose. If the ritual is performed outdoors, participants may take advantage of the natural landscape by building the sacred space so that a tree or bush guards the entryway.

Finally, an altar should be placed at the center of the sacred space, decorated with the same materials used to construct the border. Decorations are intended to remind one of the variety and beauty of nature's many shapes, forms, and textures and should be varied and colorful. Consider all senses, including the smells that will emanate from the altar when selecting decorations. The altar should hold two lit incense wands in separate stands, four unlit candles in separate candle holders placed at the north, south, east, and west sides of the altar, and a large firesafe kettle or bowl. Have chairs available for anyone who would rather sit than kneel in front of the altar.

If desired, live or recorded African drumming may play in the background throughout the ritual at a slow tempo and low volume. The music should begin at least five minutes before the ritual starts to quiet participants and set a meditative mood for the occasion.

Ritual Preparation

Each person participating brings three things to the ritual: acts for which they wish to atone written on a small sheet of paper, a personal sacrifice recorded or symbolized in a form that can be placed upon the altar (such as money, a check, a cell phone opened to a payment app, or even just a written note committing oneself to a specific act of service), and a hope for the future (unwritten). The sacrifice one is willing to make should be related to, and proportional with, either the act one atones for or the hope one has for the future. The ritual leader must be familiar with the Adinkra symbol for hope.

Adinkra symbols originated within the Akan culture of Ghana but are now used throughout the African Diaspora in textile and craft products, sculpture, furniture, and institutional, organizational, or business logos. Each symbol has a historical meaning, often reflecting a deeply held spiritual value. The most known of the Adinkra symbols is the Sankofa image, a bird symbol that conveys the importance of history and wisdom from the past. The Adinkra symbol for hope, as shown below, is shaped like two stylized hearts laid sidewise so that their tops are touching to the point of merging.

The Ritual

Individual people will vary in the ease with which they engage in the movements and positions included in this ritual. All movements and positions should be altered and assistance provided as necessary to accommodate every individual, including the option of extending the sacred space to surround a person without requiring their motion.

Demarcating the Sacred Space

The ritual leader takes a lit wand of incense from the altar and walks the entire perimeter of the ritual space clockwise, tracing a circle with the incense smoke.

A circle has no beginning and no end, and so is symbolic of the connection between all things.

Replace the wand of incense and take the second wand. Repeat tracing the circle now counterclockwise.

Smoke is visible for only a moment before becoming a part of the air surrounding us. Like smoke, our separate lives are brief before we too become a part of the enduring spirit that surrounds us.

Replace the wand of incense.

Restoring Connection

The ritual leader moves to the altar.

Morality flows from awareness of our connection with others and with nature. We lose our moral compass when we lose awareness of this connection.

Light the north, south, east, and west candles while saying:

I light one candle for each direction—north, south, east, and west—reminding us of our spiritual connection to all people in all places. These candles also symbolize the four seasons—spring, summer, fall, and winter—reminding us of our spiritual connection with all of nature.

Entering the Ritual Space

Depending on the size of the ritual space and the number of people planning to participate, the ritual leader invites one or more participants to kneel or sit in front of the guardian figure as they are able. Ensure that the space is sufficient for all to be included, regardless of their physical abilities. If the space must be extended to surround someone unable to physically enter, the following meditation will still take place prior to the circle being extended:

> You may bring no disharmony into this space. Before you enter this sacred circle, take a moment to pay attention to any thought or emotion that separates you from family, friends, community, nature, or even from your sense of who you are as a person. Think of all the people with whom you are in conflict or from whom you are disconnected. Think of all events, circumstances, or forces that seem to thwart, block, or oppose you. Take time now to address each such thought or feeling individually. To each thought or feeling that arises, say softly, "I am letting you go, as I will bring no disharmony into this space." When no further thoughts or feelings of separation well up within you, you may enter this circle.

Acts of Atonement and Sacrifice

After entering the sacred space, participants kneel or sit before the altar as they are able while the ritual leader instructs:

> In the candle flame, ignite the slip of paper on which you have written the acts for which you are atoning. Drop the paper in the bowl and let it burn completely. Let all regret, all guilt, all shame burn away, turning to ash just like the paper.

Have participants safely reignite any parts of the paper that do not burn.

Place your sacrifice on the altar. Do you affirm that what you offer in sacrifice, whether in the form of money, time, effort, or all three, is equal and proportional to what you are atoning for?

Participants affirm. Ritual leader dips a finger in the paper ash and traces, in one continuous line, the Adinkra symbol for hope on the foreheads of participants. Start the tracing in the center of the forehead, beginning from the inside of the symbol where the two halves are connected and working around to the outside of one half. Return to the central starting point and then trace the other half of the figure in the opposite direction, again ending in the center.

I trace the Adinkra symbol for hope on each of your foreheads. It is like two hearts joining to form one organ, one inseparable whole. As such, it symbolizes the deep connections you each are establishing or restoring today with these acts of atonement and sacrifice. It is meaningful that the symbol for hope is crafted from the heart, an organ that continuously beats throughout our lifetimes. It tells us that atonement is not passive. Atonement requires action on our part to be achieved, accepting responsibility for what we have done and making things right through our sacrifice. It is meaningful that the symbol for hope is the joining of hearts, for it is through connection that atonement is possible, and it is through connection that hope comes alive.

After all participants have received an Adinkra symbol, say:

Repeat after me.

Pause for repetition after each line break.

I wear the Adinkra symbol of hope on my forehead.
I accept responsibility both for what I have done
and for what I must do
to realize my hopes.
May my sacrifice remind me
that there is always hope for change.
May it be a first step
in my assuming responsibility
for the change that must come.
Through loving sacrifice, I atone,
I am forgiven,
and I am made one with all.
I am because we are.
Ashé.

Participants leave the sacred space, taking the tokens of their sacrifice from the altar to use in their daily lives.

Closing Litany

Let us close our ritual with a litany. To my call, you repeat the following response: "But through loving sacrifice all things are forgiven, and all things are one."

The ritual leader should say the response with the participants the initial few times to help them remember their part.

Call: I have lost my connection to nature.

Response: But through loving sacrifice all things are forgiven, and all things are one.

Call: I have soiled the sacred spirit of nature.

Response: But through loving sacrifice all things are forgiven, and all things are one.

Call: I have taken more than I need to sustain myself.

Response: But through loving sacrifice all things are forgiven, and all things are one.

Call: I have brought harm to other creatures when my survival did not require it.

Response: But through loving sacrifice all things are forgiven, and all things are one.

Call: I have lost my connection to others.

Response: But through loving sacrifice all things are forgiven, and all things are one.

Call: I have ignored the sacred spirit within others.

Response: But through loving sacrifice all things are forgiven, and all things are one.

Call: I have placed my needs above the needs of others.

Response: But through loving sacrifice all things are forgiven, and all things are one.

Call: I have brought harm to others when my survival did not require it.

Response: But through loving sacrifice all things are forgiven, and all things are one.

Call: I have lost my connection to myself.

Response: But through loving sacrifice all things are forgiven, and all things are one.

Call: I have ignored the sacred spirit within myself.

Response: But through loving sacrifice all things are forgiven, and all things are one.

Call: I have ignored my own needs.

Response: But through loving sacrifice all things are forgiven, and all things are one.

Call: I have brought harm to myself.

Response: But through loving sacrifice all things are forgiven, and all things are one.

Call: Ashé.

Variations

Though primarily intended for congregational settings, this ritual can also be done alone, changing the wording to the first person.

Questions for Discussion

- Can one atone for some regretted past action without the person(s) who may have experienced harm offering forgiveness?
- Does justice always require punishment and, if not, when is punishment not necessary?
- What is required for us to forgive another person?
- How can atonement occur when an entire community or group of people have suffered harm?

Discernment/Divination

Purpose

To facilitate self-evaluation, discovery, and discernment using feedback and advice from family, friends, mentors, and other trusted people.

Historical Inspiration

Divination is a part of most traditional African cultures and was brought to the African Diaspora through slavery and immigration of African peoples. African divination makes use of coins, shells, nuts, or other objects that can be cast or manipulated to yield a random pattern that leads to guidance or answers to life questions. One of the best-known divination traditions within West Africa is the *Ifá* system of the Yoruba people, but the Ibo and Fulani have similar traditions.[13] The Fon people call it *Fá*, the Luba have *Bo*, and the Ewe divination system is *Afá*. Enslaved Africans brought variations of these systems to Cuba and Brazil.

In one variation of the Ifá tradition, as an example, a specially trained priest (*babalawo*) tosses a divining chain consisting of eight half shells, each of which can independently land with its convex or concave surface pointing up. When the concave surface lands up, the babalawo makes a single mark on a divining tray. When the

13 William Russell Bascom, *Ifa Divination: Communication Between Gods and Men in West Africa* (Indiana University Press, 1991).

convex surface lands up, the babalawo marks double lines. As the chain is held in the middle and tossed so that four shells land to one side and four to the other, the babalawo obtains one of the 256 combinations in a single toss. The outcome determines which of over a thousand memorized verses the priest can recite and interpret in response to his client's question or crisis. These verses constitute a "corpus of verbal art, including myths, folk tales, praise names, incantations, songs, proverbs, and even riddles."[14] This corpus, which in 2005 the United Nations Educational, Scientific and Cultural Organization (UNESCO) included in its Masterpieces of Oral and Intangible Heritage, is the body of wisdom upon which Ifá divination depends.

One other feature of Ifá divination illustrates its genius. The babalawo divines the right verses to recite based on the random outcome of the shell toss, but the client alone has the power to select from among those verses the ones that best apply to his or her circumstances. Hence, individual autonomy and choice is a core feature of this ancient ritual. This assertion of an individual's right to choose is reminiscent of the emphasis Unitarian Universalism places on the right of individual conscience in religious and philosophical matters. The following contemporary ritual incorporates elements of African divination while utilizing the advice of family, friends, and mentors and preserving one's freedom to choose the advice to follow.

Setting and Occasion

The ritual is intended to be an annual part of a birthday celebration and can occur as part of, or instead of, receiving material gifts. It should begin before the day is given over to simply having fun.

14 Bascom, Ifa Divination.

Ritual Preparation

While the ritual occurs on or near one's birthday, preparations begin a month in advance by identifying family, friends, and mentors whose advice may guide you through the next year of life. Selecting someone for this role means you respect them and their ability to give you thoughtful and caring advice. Each person should procure a coin to give you as a tangible token of their advice. The coin should be one not easily lost or mixed up with other currency. Coins from current African nations are a decorative option, but rarely circulated US coins like silver dollars will also suffice. Ask each person to think of one thing they would wish for you to do more of, or one thing they wish you would do less of, to be happy in the year ahead.

The Ritual

On your birthday, each person you've asked offers their advice (it can be whispered if too private to say aloud). While doing so, each person gives you the coin they have selected, heads up if they are advising you to do more of something, heads down if advising you to do less. A gift may be given as well that in some way relates to the advice they offer. Accept each piece of advice graciously, giving it serious consideration, but with the understanding that you get to choose whether to follow it. Carry the coin(s) with you during a day in which you commit to following the advice.

Finally, return the coin to the giver once you believe you have either successfully implemented the advice or have determined it is not advice that will work for you. Either way, enjoy sharing the story of your attempts to follow the advice.

Variations

Birthdays are celebrated with friends and family both near and distant. Consider creating a version of this ritual to include those who are not able to be with you in person on your birthday, using coins or two-sided cards delivered by postal mail or email as part of a virtual birthday celebration.

Questions for Discussion

- Do you believe that random events like coin tosses or selecting a card from a deck can lead to useful life advice?
- What do we bring as psychological and spiritual beings to the interpretation of such random events?
- What is our responsibility when it comes to implementing the advice others offer?
- How did the accountability of knowing you must return a coin help motivate you to make life changes?

Elderhood

Purpose

To confer the special status and privilege of becoming an elder in a community.

Historical Inspiration

Elders across traditional African-derived communities occupy a position of high regard, respect, and reverence.[15] Elders are not isolated or marginalized. They are always at the center of community and family life, and their consent is often requested before community events may proceed. Their varied roles include presiding over ceremonies, serving as judges and conflict-resolvers, dividing property, creating and enforcing laws and customs, and providing guidance and wisdom to the community. To become an elder, a person must not only achieve a specified age but also be an established and respected member of the community. Traditional communities also required the potential elder to demonstrate what they considered to be good character, knowledge, wisdom, and familiarity with the customs, traditions, and history. Much like ancestorship (see Ancestorship ritual), elderhood was an earned privilege. While drawing inspiration from these traditions, contemporary adaptations must be careful to avoid ableism in elderhood rituals.

---

15 Bénezét Bujo, *The Ethical Dimension of Community: The African Model and the Dialogue between North and South* (Paulines Publications, 1998).

Occasion and Frequency

Congregations may choose a special Sunday each year to recognize and honor new elders of the community.

Setting

This ritual is appropriate for congregational settings and can be a part of a worship service.

Materials

The ritual requires a stole, preferably of kente cloth or similar African fabric.

Ritual Preparation

Congregations must decide on a process for granting the status of elder and who makes the determination. Input from both clergy and laity is important. One option would be for the minister to nominate and the congregation's board to approve. If the congregation has been naming elders for a while, a committee or council of elders might be established and given the task of choosing future elders. As noted above, elder status is granted based on age, membership, service and other contributions, character, judgment, and knowledge of the community.

The congregation should consider what privileges it wishes to confer with elderhood. This may include such ceremonial functions as lighting the chalice on special occasions, a formal request to elders present at the start of worship or other programs if the congregation may proceed, the privilege of wearing their elder stole (or a special name tag) during worship and other congregational events and meetings, free participation in congregational activities (e.g., catered social events, ticketed activities), or perhaps service on an elder council whose wisdom, advice, and institutional memory is sought when difficult or important decisions must be made.

A minister or board president should lead the ritual to communicate that the role of elder is an official status recognized within the congregation. The minister and members of the congregation who are familiar with the person's contributions should prepare a brief testimonial about what qualifies the person for elderhood.

The Ritual

Minister: It is our honor to confer the status of Congregation Elder upon [name]. This status is being conferred by virtue of [name] reaching the age of [age] and having a long history of membership and service to this community.

Include here a summary of the person's history within the congregation.

[Name] also qualifies for elder status by virtue of their character, knowledge, wisdom, and judgment amply illustrated in the following testimonials.

The minister may invite members of the congregation to give testimonial or may summarize information provided by others.

As an Elder of this congregation, you will have the following rights and privileges that we offer as a token of our gratitude and respect for your long membership and service.

Specify the privileges being conferred.

As a sign of your Elder status, the congregation is making a gift to you of this stole. Please wear it as often as you wish to events and activities within this congregation so that members, friends, and visitors will recognize you as a beloved, respected, and honored member of this community.

Place the stole on the new Elder's shoulders.

Congregation, please join me in recognizing Elder [Name].

Hug the elder or shake their hand and invite the congregation members to applaud and offer their further congratulations after the service.

Variations

The ritual may be done for one person or adapted for multiple individuals at a time. Some congregations may prefer a less ostentatious gift than a stole, but one advantage of the stole is visibility as a tangible sign of the congregation's commitment to the values embodied in the elderhood ritual. A congregation may also elect to address elders as they are addressed in some African societies using the honorific term "Baba" for male and "Nana" for female elders. These are terms commonly used for parents or grandparents and when applied to an unrelated elder are intended to convey affection and respect. If a non-gendered alternative is preferred, use the Swahili word "mzee" for "elder."

In some African American Christian churches, the term "Elder" may be given as an honorific and may be associated with various duties in the church. The term, however, may imply a hierarchy based on age that is inconsistent with the Unitarian Universalist commitment to democracy, making "Baba" and "Nana" less freighted by unwanted baggage in congregations with a diverse membership.

Questions for Discussion

- At what age should elderhood begin?
- What is the role of elders in the congregation?
- What privileges and rights should the congregation grant elders?
- In what ways are the needs of older members of the congregation considered?
- In what ways does the congregation communicate the value of elders?
- In what ways are elders marginalized in the congregation?
- How might a council of elders be utilized in congregational life?
- How does a congregation continue to treat an elder with honor and respect as their physical and/or cognitive abilities decline with age or illness?

Freedom Watch

Purpose

To honor and remember the African American struggle for freedom and justice.

Historical Inspiration

Despite his reputation as a great liberator, Abraham Lincoln used slavery emancipation as a war tactic. Lincoln issued an Emancipation Proclamation on September 22, 1862, that applied to the Confederate States, with only a threat to sign it on January 1, 1863, if they did not surrender and rejoin the Union. On New Year's Eve, free Black people gathered openly in the North, joined by their White abolitionist allies. Simultaneously, enslaved Black people gathered secretly wherever they could in the Confederate States to wait to see if the South would surrender. Five minutes before midnight, legend tells us, a man ran down the aisle of Tremont Temple Baptist Church in Boston, crying out that emancipation was coming.[16] When the Confederate States indeed did not lay down their arms, the chains of slavery begin to fall. It would take further proclamations to end slavery throughout the continent, and enslaved people in Texas did not gain their full freedom until June 19, 1865. Legend and popular accounts say that word did not reach enslaved people in Texas until June 19, 1865.

16 Kathlyn Gay, *African-American Holidays, Festivals, and Celebrations* (Omnigraphics, 2007).

Freedom celebrations occur within various African American communities at differing times of the year in association with local emancipation timelines. The two most widely known are the "Watch Night" services that occur annually in many Black churches on New Year's Eve and Juneteenth, now recognized federally and in many state and local jurisdictions on June 19th. These two commemorations are fitting bookends to the many freedom celebrations recognized within African American communities, as they mark the beginning and end of freedom's initial march. These historical events notwithstanding, African Americans continue to face the consequences of systemic, institutionalized racism. This Freedom Watch ritual commemorates both the historic and ongoing struggle for freedom.

Occasion and Frequency

We recommend performing the ritual on New Year's Eve, during Juneteenth, or on whatever date local historically enslaved African Americans gained their freedom. The ritual is intended for annual practice. It begins fifteen minutes before midnight and is precisely timed, but this may be altered if the events commemorated are expanded.

Setting

The ritual is intended for congregational practice. It can be included in a special service for Watch Night or Juneteenth that incorporates additional liturgical elements, including hymns, readings, and a sermon.

Materials

The ritual requires participation of the minister, choir, musicians, sound and light technicians (or minimally someone to lower and raise lights), and the congregation. A field song or slave holler must be selected. Ideally this will have limited verses that can be repeated softly throughout the first ten minutes of the ritual without interfering with the minister's reading. Words and music for the traditional Black anthem, "Lift Every Voice and Sing," are needed for the ritual.

Ritual Preparation

The minister, choir, musicians, and technicians will need to learn and rehearse their parts. The congregation will need instruction in advance of its response to the minister's call, including when this will be initiated. If not done in advance, the minister can cue the congregation how to respond at the beginning of the call-and-response part of the ritual.

The Ritual

The ritual begins fifteen minutes prior to midnight. The times can be changed as needed and are not rigid. The most important part of the timing is ending the spoken parts at midnight so that the bell or chime corresponds to the change of the hour.

11:45 Congregation sits silently in as near total darkness as possible.

11:46 Choir begins singing a slave song or field holler softly so that the minister can be heard above the choir. The song continues softly beneath the minister until 11:55.

11:47 **Minister:** In 1619, the ship called The White Lion brings twenty enslaved Africans ashore in Jamestown, Virginia.

11:48 In 1641, Massachusetts becomes the first colony to recognize African enslavement as legal.

11:49 In 1664, The legislatures of Maryland, New Jersey, the Carolinas, New York, and Virginia make enslavement perpetual for African people within their state borders.

11:50 In 1705, the Virginia Slave Code allows enslavers to torture the people they enslave without fear of legal repercussion and rewards the recapture of African people who escape to freedom.

11:51 The Negro Act of 1740 forbids the education and assembly of enslaved African people.

11:52 In 1793, Congress makes it a crime to aid or interfere in the arrest of enslaved African people who escape to freedom.

11:53 In 1794, the invention of the cotton gin increases the demand for more African people to enslave for their labor.

11:54 In the 1857 Dred Scott v. Sandford case, the United States Supreme Court rules African Americans are not citizens of the United States and forbids Congress to prohibit African enslavement in any federal territory.

11:55 Choir stops singing and begins chanting: Emancipation is coming! Emancipation is coming! as lights come up gradually to full illumination.

11:56 Choir stops chanting. Music to the anthem "Lift Every Voice and Sing" begins (without lyrics).

11:57 Begin minister's call and congregation's response.

Minister: In 1676, poor Whites and Black people unite in rebellion in Virginia.

Congregation: The struggle continues today.

Minister: In 1688, Pennsylvania Quakers adopt the first formal antislavery resolution in American history.

Congregation: The struggle continues today.

Minister: In 1739, enslaved Africans lead the Stono Rebellion in Florida.

Congregation: The struggle continues today.

Minister: In 1775, the Pennsylvania Society for the Abolition of Slavery is founded.

Congregation: The struggle continues today.

Minister: In 1793, Massachusetts becomes the first state to abolish slavery.

Congregation: The struggle continues today.

Minister: In 1800, Gabriel Prosser plans the first major rebellion against slavery with 1000 Black people joining him in Virginia.

Congregation: The struggle continues today.

Minister: In 1808, trading enslaved African people is banned in the United States and all British colonies.

Congregation: The struggle continues today.

Minister: In 1816, freeborn and emancipated Black people begin leaving America to create an African colony that became the Republic of Liberia.

Congregation: The struggle continues today.

Minister: In 1831, Nat Turner led a rebellion of 75 enslaved Africans in the United States.

Congregation: The struggle continues today.

Minister: In 1839, Africans aboard the ship Amistad revolted against their enslavement, eventually taking their case to the Supreme

Court, which affirmed both their right to freedom and their right to resist enslavement.

Congregation: The struggle continues today.

Minister: In 1859, John Brown's raid on Harper's Ferry Armory put America on the road to Civil War over slavery.

Congregation: The struggle continues today.

Minister: In 1863, the bravery of the all-Black 54th Massachusetts Volunteer Infantry fighting in the Civil War and the work of Frederick Douglass and other abolitionists forces Abraham Lincoln to finally sign the Emancipation Proclamation, ending slavery in America.

Congregation: The struggle continues today.

Minister: In 1865, Congress ratifies a Constitutional amendment to abolish slavery throughout the US

Congregation: The struggle continues today.

Midnight Music stops. A bell or chime rings twelve times to mark the time. Music resumes and choir leads the congregation in singing "Lift Every Voice and Sing."

The ritual concludes with a celebration after the service.

Variations

To accommodate families, congregations may consider practicing the ritual earlier so that children may participate. Elements of the ritual can be frightening for young children. Congregations may want to consider a separate intergenerational observance that reduces the more dramatic elements that take place in the dark.

The timeline included in the ritual may leave out events that are important in your region or location. Consider adding or substituting these events in the ritual. Some congregations may wish to emphasize the role of Unitarian Universalists in the history of enslavement and emancipation and may alter the events listed accordingly. Different songs and music may be used if desired, as long as they similarly evoke the emotions of sadness and lament during the first ten minutes and provide emotional uplift and inspiration during the remainder of the ritual.

Questions for Discussion

- What is the history of enslavement of African people in the local area or region?
- What was the impact of enslavement on your family, either as a White or a Black American?
- How does the legacy of enslavement continue to impact you today?
- Why is it important to remember and commemorate the history of enslavement?

Grief Release

This ritual is not intended to be a substitute for mental health or ministerial intervention. If your grief persists or if you are feeling suicidal, you should seek professional assistance.

Purpose

To experience and then release grief so that life may resume.

Historical Inspiration

Malidoma and Sobonfu Somé, writers and spiritual teachers who promoted cross-cultural adoption of African spiritual practices, describe Dagara grief rituals in several of their books.[17] Similar practices are abundant across African and the African Diasporan cultures. Most of these grief rituals are associated with funeral practices, though the Somés' adaptation of Dagara rituals for Western participants apply to grief broadly. While funeral and memorial services are outside of the scope of our book, they provide a context for the ritual that follows. We summarize some phases of African funerals that are relevant to this grief ritual.

First, African funeral rituals encourage full acknowledgement, experience, and open expression of grief, typically while the body is

17 Malidoma Patrice Somé, *Ritual Power, Healing, and Community* (Penguin, 1997).
Sobonfu E. Somé, *Falling Out of Grace: Meditations on Loss, Healing and Wisdom* (North Bay Books, 2003).

still at home. The family will wash the body before removing it from the home. Mirrors are covered or turned to face the wall, the body is taken out feet first, and a circuitous route is taken to where the body will be interred. These efforts are intended to prevent the person's spirit from seeing itself and from knowing the way back to its corporeal home, as otherwise it may return and interfere with the living. It is essential that all family and community members participate in the funeral, which can go on for days depending upon the status of the deceased. Music plays an integral role in encouraging and channeling emotional catharsis. In some traditions, the family will not accompany the body to where it is to be interred, trusting this to others. A community feast and celebration of the deceased's transition follows.

Generalizing from these funeral rites, the key elements of grief release in the African and African Diaspora traditions include emotional catharsis through music, cleansing and removal of the body, the symbolic rearranging of one's environment, burial, community participation, and celebration of the transition.

Occasion and Frequency

As the process of grieving cannot be rushed, this ritual may occur as often as needed to release grief.

Setting

This ritual is intended for home settings.

Materials

This ritual requires a disposable container for your grief, digging tools for burying the grief, and words and music that evoke your feelings.

Ritual Preparation

It is important to schedule enough time to allow yourself to fully feel and express your grief. Consult with people you trust on how long you may need, leaving generous leeway in case it takes longer than you expect. If you spend this time grieving alone, make sure others are checking in on you regularly to ensure your emotional safety as you allow yourself to grieve. When you and trusted advisors believe it is time to begin the process of releasing your grief, the celebratory phases of the ritual may be added.

The Ritual

Alone, or with trusted family and friends, allow yourself to feel and express your grief fully and completely. Describe the source of your grief and how you experience it emotionally and physically, using your own written or spoken words or ones borrowed from other sources. Grief may also be expressed in movement and dance. Play and listen to the music that seems most evocative and expressive of your grief, perhaps pulling from a wide range of musical styles. Consider creating a playlist for yourself or others that best captures your experience of grief. Allow yourself to cry, to sleep, or to sit silently with your grief. Take your grief with you on a walk. Do what is needed to feel your grief, rather than avoid, deny, hide, or dull it.

Once it is time, cleanse yourself fully. Bathe alone or allow an intimate partner or a close family member to bathe you. Imagine soap and water washing away the grief. Soak in water, imagining the grief being drawn out and absorbed. Release the grief-filled water into the drain but capture a part of it in a container.

Once dry and clothed, cover all mirrors and curtain the windows in the home. Cover the grief container as well so it is in complete darkness. Remove the grief from the home to a place where it can be buried. As it exits the door, say:

> Grief, I release you in darkness, permitting you to leave and permitting myself to begin to move on.

Dig a hole and pour the water of grief into the soil. While burying it, you or another person can recite:

> Grief, I bury you here so that I may begin to move on. Though I shall never forget what I have lost, I allow myself to release you. I carry my cherished memories, I carry that which I shall always love within me, as I release you and move on.

Destroy the container in an environmentally appropriate manner and permanently discard it.

Your grief now released, open the curtains and uncover the mirrors. Rearrange furniture or routines to symbolize the start of your transition from grieving. Celebrate this transition in a party with family and friends, publicly acknowledging your release of your grief and asking their support in moving through this transition.

Variations

If you wish others to witness your cleansing, consider speaking your grief into a container of water as an alternative to bathing, or washing only your face. You can remove and bury the grief yourself, or if you wish to have no association with it, give it to another person to perform these parts of the ritual.

If you want to visit your grief again or expect it to return, bury it close by so that you can reengage it as needed, knowing it is healthy to accept your feelings rather than attempting to suppress them. Return to and repeat parts of this ritual when and as often as needed to release grief again. Alternatively, it can be buried far away or even in a place unknown to you when you believe you are ready to release it for good.

The depth of burial can be a few inches to a few feet, depending upon whatever depth feels right given the source and nature of your grief. Ask for assistance digging the hole if needed, even if you wish to place the grief and begin burying it alone. The assistant can then return to finish filling the hole as needed.

Adapt this ritual for griefs that are shared by multiple people so that they may be jointly released.

Questions for Discussion

- What role does grief play in my life?
- How can my community of family and friends support both my grieving and my release of grief?
- How do I know when my grief is so great that I need mental health intervention, ministerial support, or both?

Healing

Purpose

To marshal the energy to heal from physical, psychological, or spiritual wounds.

Historical Inspiration

Traditional healing in Africa bears only partial resemblance to contemporary Western medicine. Among the Yoruba, illness is traditionally treated by diviners, herbalists, and priests, whose knowledge encompasses various remedies and rituals to ward off ill health.[18] The Basaa people distinguish "ordinary" and "extraordinary" health conditions. Ordinary conditions (e.g., influenza or a bone fracture) that affect only the body may be treated by doctors, nurses, or paraprofessionals. In contrast, extraordinary health conditions involve a spiritual component requiring not only medical care but also the services of a specialized healer.[19] Extraordinary diseases do not just afflict single individuals; they impact the family and community. Even noncontagious diseases spread through a network of people to become a whole community problem. Healing rituals are not just for the individual who has fallen ill but are also intended to bring comfort and healing to the larger circle of people who are impacted.

18 M. E. Peek, "Traditional African medicine," *The Pharos* 58, no. 2 (Spring 1995).

19 S. B. Mandeng, "*Traditional Healing of a 'Non-ordinary' Disease (Kon) Among the Basaa of Cameroun: A Religious-Anthropological Approach*" (unpublished doctoral dissertation, Emory University, 1984).

Traditional priests perform healing rituals in recognition of an intimate connection between the health of the spirit and the health of the body. The goal of such rituals isn't necessarily to cure a physical disease but rather to restore a sense of spiritual well-being, regardless of whether the physical disease remains. Medicine cures, but ritual heals. Healing may occur even when medicine fails to cure. Healing may occur even when medical intervention fails to prevent death or disability.

Music (especially drumming), singing, and dance are an integral part of the healing. African healing rituals also offer an opportunity to resolve grievances that may contribute to the person's ill health and to reaffirm love and commitment to their well-being. Every person with a grievance has an opportunity to speak and resolve it, ending with the assertion, *So it was, but no longer is.* Once all grievances are resolved, those assembled are led in a recitation of blessings intended to defeat the sickness and to affirm the community's commitment to the person's recovery.

Within the African American Pentecostal tradition, we see the influence of traditional African approaches to healing. William J. Seymour, the son of former slaves and an itinerant minister, began holding prayer meetings in the early 1900s that became known as the Azusa Street Revival. Seymour's services attracted as many as 1,500 worshippers of all ethnic backgrounds and socioeconomic strata to participate as equals in services that could last a day or longer. Newspapers of the day were highly critical of the spectacle of an undifferentiated mass of people who otherwise might never encounter one another, suddenly on equal footing and engaged in an unabated frenzy of dancing, shouting, singing, praying, trance, and instantaneous healing of all manner of sickness and disability.[20]

20 Jack W. Hayford and S. David Moore, *The Charismatic Century: The Enduring Impact of the Azusa Street Revival* (Warner Faith, 2006).

More recently, Western physicians have developed interest in alternative and complementary approaches to healing that work alongside and enhance evidence-based treatments. In 1992, the National Institutes of Health (NIH), the federal agency that funds most medical research in the US, created the Office of Alternative Medicine, now known as the National Center for Complementary and Integrative Health. This branch of NIH has disbursed millions of dollars in grant money to universities across the country to study alternative and complementary medical treatments for a variety of health conditions. It also conducts its own research into health issues such as chronic pain.

Some general conclusions emerged across dozens of completed studies:

- It helps to get rest.
- It helps to hear music.
- It helps to be touched.
- It helps to imagine your own healing.
- It helps to know people care.
- It helps to have a larger purpose in life, even when you are ill.

All six of these elements are present in traditional healing in the African Diaspora and can be incorporated in the ritual that follows singly or in combination.

Some aspects of this ritual refer to healing from acute conditions, such as broken bones and other diseases. People with chronic or terminal conditions may wish to adapt it to better suit their individual situations. For more on this, see Variations.

Occasion and Frequency

The ritual is performed whenever healing is necessary and as frequently as needed to achieve a sense of well-being.

Setting

The setting and location are flexible and can be adapted to home, church, hospital, or other community settings.

Materials

Materials to gather include music, soap and water for bathing, and oil for massaging. In some African cultures, a red sheet is placed beneath the person being healed and a white sheet is used to cover them. Candles are placed near the head and feet.

Ritual Preparation

Preparation for this ritual consists of scheduling time and people. Set aside time for yourself to rest, listen to music, and perform other solitary parts of the ritual. You (or someone handling logistics for you) will also need to organize a time in which other people can show their care and concern over your healing. The psychological impact of this ritual is derived significantly from knowing that people are pausing the course of their lives to be with you, in varyingly intimate, emotional, and meaningful ways, and focusing their care and concern on you. This includes people with whom you may have been in previous conflict. You and those with whom you have an ongoing or past conflict should only participate in this ritual together when all parties agree to let the ritual be the ending point of the conflict.

For the touch portion of the ritual, participants should be people with whom you are most intimately and emotionally connected because they will be in direct physical contact. Participants must also be mature, able to give free consent, and empowered to withdraw consent at any time. On the day of the ritual, dress comfortably, in garments or coverings that allow as much direct contact with the skin as personal comfort permits. This will vary with your degree of intimacy with those present.

If using candles during a communal part of the ritual, ensure ahead of time that none of the participants have allergies to scents or to smoke. Unscented candles or battery-operated ones are less likely to cause health concerns for participants.

The Ritual

Rest

Schedule time to sit or lay without activity, time away from television, radio, reading, internet surfing, texting, social media, and talking. The moment can occur indoors or outdoors. What is essential is that you are engaged in no activity other than resting and allowing the body to devote its energy to restoring itself. Even when you have eliminated external stimulation, it is easy to allow mental activity to fill in. To keep your thoughts focused on healing rest, mentally chant the following litany:

> I am surrounded by the spirit of nature.
> May it fill me.
> I lay in the cradle of nature.
> May it give me rest.
> I live by the law of nature.
> May it protect me.
> I feed from the womb of nature.
> May it replenish me.
> I am aware of the spirit of nature.
> May it heal me.

Music

Listen to music that impacts you emotionally. Listen to music that engages and focuses your mind. This may be the music of your youth or a new musical genre you have just discovered. It may be music that makes you sit and reflect or music that moves you to dance. It may be beautiful, melancholy, or joyous—whatever you prefer. The critical factor is that the music engages you fully. Alternate music and rest or play music during rest that quiets and calms the mind.

Touch

Sit or recline comfortably, with one or more candles at your feet and head. Maintain dim, subdued lighting—perhaps only using candlelight—and play soft, slow instrumental music. Participants can offer different forms of touch based on your mutual comfort. Touch can include clasping hands; stroking the forehead or arm; gently massaging whatever part of the body feels comfortable to you; washing your feet, hands, face, or hair; softly rubbing a scented oil into your skin or hair, or any other form of touch that is mutually agreeable and welcome. Continue providing a healing touch as long as mutually desired. One option to indicate the end of the ritual is with a pleasant sound, such as a bell or a singing bowl.

Imagine Healing

While the immune system benefit to imagining your body attacking and overcoming disease may be minor, meditation can make pain and discomfort more tolerable. Assume a comfortable sitting or reclining position. Breathe in while imagining yourself filling up with an energy capable of destroying, removing, or diminishing whatever afflicts your body. Use whatever image works best—fire, water, wind, light, or any other symbol of energy and power. Draw in this energy as you breathe, chanting silently:

> Ancestral spirits, fill me with the power to burn away [or wash away, blow away, obliterate, melt, remove, etc.] my illness [or headache, infection, cancer, etc.].

If there is a particular ancestor who was in a health or healing profession, it may help to visualize them and to invoke this ancestor's name in the chant.

Holding your breath, imagine this energy flowing to the affected part of your body. As you imagine directing this energy to where it is needed, chant:

> Ancestral spirits, burn away my [disease/condition].

As you try to experience what this would feel like, imagine the sensation of the disease or condition being burned, melted, washed, or blown away. Exhale as you imagine the disease's elimination from your body with the outgoing air.

> Ancestral spirits, remove and expel what keeps me from healing.

Repeat these chants in association with your breath several times.

When ready to begin the concluding cycle of breaths, inhale imagining yourself filling up with a soothing, comforting energy. Again, use whatever image you find soothing and healing—a balm, warm or cool water, a gentle breeze, a soft glow.

> Ancestral spirits, fill me with the energy to soothe and heal my body.

Hold the breath, directing the soothing sensation to whatever part of the body needs healing or to the entire body. Exhale. Repeat these soothing breaths several times.

Reconciliation

Make peace with family or friends you have quarreled with. Having the participation of people with whom you have reconciled during the final caring part of the ritual increases its emotional impact. Peacemaking can occur in individually arranged sessions or, even more powerfully, at a time when all who have had troubled relations can come at once to make peace with you.

Whether done on individual dates or in one common gathering, peacemaking is a private meditation between two people, with a third person acting as facilitator if needed. A facilitator is especially important if the conflict between the two is still raw and painful and there is potential for the interaction to go badly. Either person should feel free to request that a third person be present to remind the two to maintain the safe format of the ritual—or to end the ritual if it might do harm rather than heal. In no case should the ritual take place without the advance agreement of both parties, and either should be free to end the ritual at any time. If peacemaking fails, it can be tried again later.

Peacemaking begins with the two people greeting and embracing. If they have not seen one another in some time, they may begin with a more casual conversation to relate what has happened to each since they were last together. Once this is done, each should rest comfortably but close enough that they may easily grasp one another's hands. Light a single candle and dim all other lighting. Clasp hands, close eyes, and begin chanting together softly:

Ancestral spirits, make us one again.

Continue chanting aloud until the person being healed elects to fall silent. The other person should then also become silent and the chanting continue silently. Again, the focus person signals when it is time to stop, this time with a squeeze of the hands. Each person opens eyes to face one another, hands still clasped.

The person coming to restore the relationship (the Peacemaker) speaks first, while the person being healed listens. The Peacemaker should come prepared to say, in succinct, single sentences, the actions they have done that strained the relationship. This is not intended to be a confession or an admission of guilt. It is only an acknowledgment of one's role in damaging the relationship. Each statement begins:

Peacemaker: Whether I intended to or not, I have lost my connection with you by . . .

The choices for ending the above phrase are infinite. They can vary from frank admissions of guilt, if that is what is felt (e.g., *by betraying your trust, by cheating on you, by putting my needs before yours*), to simple acknowledgments of the break in the relationship (e.g., *by staying away, by no longer trying to work things out, by giving up on our relationship*). When the Peacemaker feels particularly hurt and wronged, the ending can simply be an acknowledgment of the pain that has kept the two apart (e.g., *by not being able to forget, by not forgiving, by needing to protect myself*).

To each of the above statements, the person undergoing healing has only one response:

So it was, but no longer is.

The Peacemaker offers as many such statements as they wish to fully cover what has separated the two people and to bring about a restoration of the relationship. When all statements have been made, the Peacemaker ends by echoing the response of the person being healed:

So it was, but no longer is.

At this point, the two people reverse roles.

Person being healed: Whether I intended to, or not, I have lost my connection with you by . . .

Peacemaker: So it was, but no longer is.

When all statements are made, the person being healed closes as before by echoing the Peacemaker's last response,

So it was, but no longer is.

The two embrace again. While holding the embrace, the Peacemaker whispers in the person's ear,

Peacemaker: In the presence of our ancestors, we are restored and may you be healed.

Person being healed: In the presence of our ancestors, we are restored and may I be healed.

The embrace ends and both say together,

Ashé.

There should be no further conversation about the conflict and no further attempts at settling or resolving issues. The two people should not speak about the conflict again. It is over. If there is some lingering legal dispute, then it is left in the hands of others to resolve. If done in a communal gathering, the Peacemaker leaves and a new Peacemaker comes in after an interval of time sufficient for the person being healed to regain composure and readiness. A facilitator can be valuable in spacing the ritual out so that one session does not carry over into another. When all conflicts have been resolved, shift the gathering into a celebration of restored connection with broad and joyful participation of family, friends, and community. The ill person participates as their energy and strength allow.

Receiving Care

We often say to those who are suffering that we will pray for them. Others will say that we are keeping the person in our thoughts and are sending them "positive energy." There is no undisputed evidence that praying for another person (or keeping them in your thoughts) helps cure disease. The real power of healing thoughts and prayers may lie in the knowledge that others care. Knowing that others care for us can be healing.

The following part of the ritual optionally uses a red sheet to lie upon and a white sheet to cover you. Place candles at your head and feet. Schedule a time when all participants in the healing can be present in person or remotely. Even if not all are physically present, it can be beneficial to know that at this moment, people far and near are pausing to think of you and to recite their part of the litany, even if you cannot hear them and they cannot hear you. This part of the ritual affirms the goodness of life despite illness, absolves you of the undeserved guilt people often feel about becoming ill, and affirms love and forgiveness as a part of healing.

One

Call: After each call, please respond with "May I be healed." Spirit of nature, bring healing to [Name].

Response: May I be healed.

Call: Ancestral spirits, we invoke you to heal [Name].

Response: May I be healed.

Call: Like the red sheet below you, may sickness be left behind.

Response: May I be healed.

Call: Like the white sheet above you, may health be ahead.

Response: May I be healed.

Call: Candles at your feet, draw out all sickness.

Response: May I be healed.

Call: Candles at your crown, draw in energy and life.

Response: May I be healed.

Two

Call: After each call, please respond with "I love and am loved." You do not bear this illness alone.

Response: I love and am loved.

Call: We who care bear illness with you.

Response: I love and am loved.

Call: We are near and we are far.

Response: I love and am loved.

Call: Distance is no barrier to our love.

Response: I love and am loved.

Call: We who care are always here.

Response: I love and am loved.

Call: You and we are one in our love.

Response: I love and am loved.

Three

Call: After each call, please respond with "I forgive and am forgiven." What is done cannot be undone.

Response: I forgive and am forgiven.

Call: We did not know this would happen.

Response: I forgive and am forgiven.

Call: We did not wish this to happen.

Response: I forgive and am forgiven.

Call: We did not make this happen.

Response: I forgive and am forgiven.

Call: We cannot change what has happened.

Response: I forgive and am forgiven.

Call: We change what we can, and together go on.

Response: I forgive and am forgiven.

Four

Call: After each call, please respond with "May I live it well." We know that life is fragile.

Response: May I live it well.

Call: We know that life is fleeting.

Response: May I live it well.

Call: Life brings pain as surely as it brings peace.

Response: May I live it well.

Call: Life brings sadness as surely as it brings joy.

Response: May I live it well.

Call: Life alternates between good times and bad.

Response: May I live it well.

Call: But at its core life is good.

Response: May I live it well.

In the following section, the person undergoing healing can choose from several options or combine them. Their choice may also change over time as their medical condition and treatment goals evolve.

Five

Call: After each call, please respond with "May I be [chosen response]." Healing takes its many forms.

Response: May I be restored / determined / accepting / at peace.

Call: Healing may come as a restoration of health.

Response: May I be restored / determined / accepting / at peace.

Call: Healing may come as a determination to fight.

Response: May I be restored / determined / accepting / at peace.

Call: Healing may come as an acceptance of what is.

Response: May I be restored / determined / accepting / at peace.

Call: Healing may come as peace with what is to be.

Response: May I be restored / determined / accepting / at peace.

Call: May healing come to you in the form you desire.

Response: May I be restored / determined / accepting / at peace.

Optionally, repeat the above litany one or more times, pausing thirty seconds between each repetition. After the last repetition, pause ten seconds, and end together with *Ashé!* Remote participants unable to continue for all agreed repetitions should complete at least one full cycle, then end by saying *Ashé* while other participants continue. Repeat the caring ritual as often as is practical and desired. Wash the sheets each time, and replace candles as needed.

Larger Purpose

Healing may leave little time, motivation, or energy for work. If you can work, do only the work tasks that truly matter. If you are in quarantine, this may be the opportunity to do the project you have been unable to find time for or to step away from work entirely and focus on a domestic task that has been long postponed. If you are facing a debilitating or fatal condition, then you have no time to waste on the trivial. The work that has meaning to you may have nothing to do with your career. You may choose to paint, to write, to travel, to spend time with loved ones, to tell your most precious stories to your children or grandchildren, etc. The point is to not waste your time with what doesn't matter. If you only have time and energy for minutes of purposeful work per day, those minutes should be spent wisely in full cognizance of their preciousness.

It is rumored that even on his deathbed, the great Albert Einstein was still doing the calculations for a theory he could never complete. His work mattered, even at the end.

Variations

Not all parts of the ritual will apply to every person and situation. A lingering cold may only require rest, while a bout of pneumonia may benefit from the imaginative healing part of the ritual. Choose the parts that are important in your own healing and in the healing of others who are going through the experience with you.

Not all illnesses and conditions are equally serious. You would not necessarily expect to resolve all conflicts and disputes during a mild flu from which you are likely to fully recover. A terminal cancer diagnosis, however, might move you to engage in resolving breaches in relationships. Similarly, not all instances require a facilitator be included in the ritual, but as the seriousness of the condition increases so too does the benefit of having a facilitator on hand to help both with arrangements and with the conduct of the ritual. Facilitators may be ministers, other religious or healing professionals, or laity.

People living with chronic illness may want to replace the parts of the ritual that focus on a return to full health with ones that acknowledge the strength and resilience of adapting to chronic health conditions. For example, in the Imagining Healing section, you could replace the requests for ancestral healing with ones like these:

Ancestral spirits, fill me with the energy to carry on through my condition. Ancestral spirits, still the churning waters of my heart. Ancestral spirits, help me find new ways of thriving. Ancestral spirits, soothe my body and bring me peace.

Questions for Discussion

- What does healing mean to me?
- What does my healing mean to my loved ones?
- When have I experienced healing?
- How do I understand the difference between cure and healing?

Karamu

Purpose

The Swahili word *karamu* translates literally to "supper." This translation, however, does not convey the centrality of food and food-related ritual in African and African Diasporic cultures. Food is used to convey welcome and hospitality, to create feelings of unity and joy, to celebrate current and historical accomplishments, and to embody sacred principles of faith.

Historical Inspiration

Meal-related rituals are likely as old as humanity and, consequently, have no single point of historical origin. Two historical events are important, however, in contemporary African American karamu rituals. Maulana Ndabezitha Karenga (born Ronald Everett), Professor and Chair of Africana Studies at California State University, introduced the Kwanzaa holiday in 1966 (see Kwanzaa ritual). Celebrated annually from December 26 to January 1, the holiday climaxes with a grand celebration that often includes a communal feast. With as many as 2 million African Americans observing the holiday, Kwanzaa spread the idea of African-inspired feasts in the African American community.[21] Brother Edward Simms Jr. created a feast he called the Umoja Karamu in 1971 as a means of strengthening the unity within

---

21 Keith A. Mayes, *Kwanzaa: Black Power and the Making of the African American Holiday Tradition* (Routledge, 2009).

Black families.[22] While initially celebrated in the Temple of the Black Messiah in Washington, DC, on the fourth Sunday of November, the Umoja Karamu spread to African American communities in the northern cities of Baltimore, Chicago, Detroit, and Philadelphia.

Occasion and Frequency

While the Umoja Karamu and Kwanzaa feasts occur in November and December, respectively, community feasts are a welcome inclusion in any holiday observance. An African-inspired cultural feast may occur as often as church potlucks.

Setting

Karamu may be held in home, congregational, or community settings.

Materials

The Karamu ritual uses five tablecloths or place mats, respectively colored black, white, red, green, and gold (yellow is an acceptable substitute for gold). Also gather five candles in candle holders, either in these same colors or all black. Food dishes should be prepared that match these colors as closely as possible, with at least one food dish in each color (e.g., black-eyed peas, white rice, red tomatoes, collard greens, golden fried or curried chicken). Finally, five small, empty bowls, all in one color, are needed to hold a poured libation during the ritual and a glass or goblet containing wine or other beverage.

The largest expense is for food and meal furnishings, and the cost can be managed by distributing them across participants. The classic church potluck is a low-cost option that also allows each participant to control their own expense.

22 Kathlyn Gay, *African-American Holidays, Festivals, and Celebrations* (Omnigraphics, 2007).

Ritual Preparation

The tablecloths or mats should be arranged in separate areas in order (black, white, red, green, and gold) across one or more tables, along with the corresponding candles. Each area should be large enough to accommodate food dishes of the corresponding color, the corresponding candle, and a libation bowl. One person can facilitate the ritual, doing all the speaking parts, or it can be divided between as many as five people. The food blessing at the end may be done by a minister or a layperson.

The Ritual

The ritual begins after the table is set and food is placed.

> Let us gather around our communal table. Each area symbolizes an era of African American history.
>
> Light the candle in the black area.
>
> The black area of our table reminds us of our time before slavery when we lived in peace and freedom in Africa. I pour a libation to our African Ancestors, known and unknown, from that era.
>
> Pour a libation in the bowl in the black area of the table.
> Light the candle in the white area.
>
> The white area of our table reminds us of our time of enslavement, a time we must remember so that we never lose our love for freedom and justice. I pour a libation to our enslaved ancestors whose strength, cunning, and courage we honor still. If you know the names of enslaved ancestors, either hereditary or communally shared, I invite you to say them now.

Pour a libation in the bowl in the white area.
Light the candle in the red area.

The red area of our table reminds us of our past and ongoing eras of struggle for freedom, justice, and equity in all its forms. Just as we have struggled here at home, we unite with all who struggle throughout the world to make these ideals a living reality. I pour a libation to all who have fought for freedom, justice, and equity. Say their names as I pour this libation.

Pour a libation in the bowl in the red area.
Light the candle in the green area.

The green area of our table reminds us of our past and present victories over racism; our achievements despite injustice; and our ability, time and again, to make a way out of no way. I pour a libation to all those who have overcome and are overcoming. Say their names as I pour this libation.

Pour a libation in the bowl in the green area.
Light the candle in the gold area.

The gold area of our table reminds us of our enduring dreams and our unceasing hope for the future. While we may experience setbacks and disappointments, we will never know defeat. I pour a libation to all who dream and hope and to all those in our history and our lives who inspire and sustain our belief in the future. Say their names as I pour this final libation.

Pour a libation in the bowl in the gold area.

Let us now bless this food . . . (see Meditation and Prayer rituals).

After the blessing, the food is shared.

Variations

A UU chalice may be used as a central flame from which the candles are lit. In addition to choosing foods by color, foods can be prepared using recipes from historical periods referenced in the ritual. Consider incorporating recipes from throughout Africa and the African Diaspora. After removing the main and side dishes, desserts corresponding to each color (e.g., chocolate cake, vanilla ice cream, red velvet cake, pistachio ice cream, yellow cake) may be placed on the serving table. During or after the meal, consider sharing stories of the people who were named during each libation, especially if they are personal, hereditary ancestors who may not be known to everyone. Consider mindful eating during a part of the meal, when you intentionally slow your consumption and focus on every sensation you experience—the sight, smell, taste, texture, and sound of food as it is consumed.

Questions for Discussion

- What role does food play in your personal, family, community, and religious life?
- What family food rituals have you known over your life?
- In what ways do your food choices reflect your values and ideals?
- What was it like to be reminded of past, present, and future times in African American history?
- What changes in foods popular with African Americans have occurred over time, and what does this reflect about the conditions in which we have lived?
- What does it mean to you to refer to African American cuisine as soul food?

Kwanzaa

Purpose

Kwanzaa is a pan-African celebration of the successes or "fruits" of the year that incorporates traditional African cultural elements and values. Though inspired by African harvest festivals, the holiday is the product of African American creativity.

Historical Inspiration

Maulana Ndabezitha Karenga (born Ronald Everett) created the holiday in 1966. Karenga was active in the Student Nonviolent Coordinating Committee and the Congress on Racial Equality before creating his own Black Nationalist organization. This organization had violent clashes with the Black Panther Party, and Karenga served time in prison. This appeared to be a turning point in his life. While in prison and on parole in the 1970s, Karenga published essays, earned several doctorates, and began an academic career. Dr. Karenga became a professor and the Chair of Africana Studies at California State University.

The name Kwanzaa is derived from a Swahili phrase meaning "first fruits." Kwanzaa celebrates the fruits or successes of the year in addition to the *Nguzo Saba*, or Seven Principles (also referred to as a Black Values System), which Karenga developed during his community activist years. Each day of Kwanzaa is devoted to one of the principles. The seven Kwanzaa principles in their order of celebration are *umoja* (unity), *kujichagulia* (self-determination), *ujima* (collective work and responsibility), *ujamaa* (cooperative economics), *nia* (purpose), *kuumba* (creativity), and *imani* (faith). A longer definition of each principle is incorporated in the ritual litany that follows.

Estimates are that 0.5 to 2 million people celebrate Kwanzaa in the US and other parts of the African Diaspora, including in Black communities in Canada, France, Great Britain, Jamaica, and Brazil.[23] Numerous US stamps commemorate Kwanzaa, and the poet Maya Angelou narrated a 2009 documentary on Kwanzaa entitled *The Black Candle.*

Occasion and Frequency

Kwanzaa is celebrated annually from December 26 to January 1.

Setting

Kwanzaa celebrations occur at home as well as in congregational and community settings.

Materials

The Kwanzaa accoutrements are highly symbolic and begin with a straw mat (the *mkeka* in Swahili) that represents tradition and serves as the foundation upon which all holiday objects rest, symbolically indicating how all things rest upon tradition. Placed upon the mkeka are one or more ears of corn (the *muhinde*) corresponding to the number of children in the family. Even when there are no children, one ear of corn is placed to represent the potential for children. A bowl of fruit and vegetables (*bakuli la matunda na mboga*) also rests on the mkeka. These fruits and vegetables of the harvest represent the year's

23 Mayes, *Kwanzaa.*

successes. A communal or unity cup (the *kikombe cha umoja*) is placed on the mat for pouring and drinking libations. The centerpiece is a seven-branched candelabrum (the *kinara*) with three red (placed to the left of center), one black (placed at center), and three green (placed right of center) candles (the *mishumaa saba*) to represent each of the seven principles. Though not a requirement, paper or cloth posters with each of the seven principles printed and defined are often included.

All materials are displayed on a table in the home or community setting throughout Kwanzaa. These materials may be obtained separately, but the popularity of the holiday has led to many commercially available Kwanzaa sets that come complete with all necessary materials. There also are Kwanzaa-themed stories and music available for purchase. Participants may wish to dress in African-style clothing or wear African jewelry and hair styles. Presents are exchanged within families. Handcrafted, personal gifts are preferred, but Kwanzaa was also planned for participants to take advantage of after-Christmas holiday sales. Kwanzaa additionally provides an opportunity to patronize African American businesses or African artisans and craftspeople. A gift of African art or crafts is particularly appropriate during Kwanzaa.

Ritual Preparation

The Kwanzaa table should be assembled on or before the first day of Kwanzaa. To promote understanding of the holiday and its symbols, make this a family or community affair, with multiple people contributing to creating the table. The unity cup should be filled with wine or another beverage just prior to the candle lighting ritual. Plan activities in advance consistent with each Kwanzaa principle. Schedule time when the family or community group can gather in the evening for the candle lighting and discussion. December 31 is devoted to kuumba (creativity) during the day, but this can also extend to a later New Year's Eve celebration that showcases Black creativity. This evening celebration also typically includes a feast (see Karamu), which must be planned and prepared. The Kwanzaa candle lighting, however, replaces the Karamu ritual. January 1, the final day of Kwanzaa, centers on faith and typically is spent in quiet, spiritual reflection at home or in congregational settings.

The Ritual

Kwanzaa is celebrated by performing an activity consistent with the principle of the day. Here are examples of two activities for each day of Kwanzaa for a Unitarian Universalist or other religious congregation, one focused inward on the congregation and the other outward to the larger community.

December 26	**Umoja** (Unity)	**Inward:** Covenant group members meet to commit to ways they will be available in the coming year to respond to each other's needs. **Outward:** Congregation partners with members of another faith on a project or social justice issue for the purpose of finding common ground.
December 27	**Kujichagulia** (Self-determination)	**Inward:** Youth group meets to strategize ways it can make its voice heard in the congregation. **Outward:** Congregation board commits to supporting businesses in the coming year that are owned by individuals identifying as Black, female, or LGBTQI+.

December 28	**Ujima** (Collective Work and Responsibility)	**Inward:** Congregation members spend a day cleaning or repairing church property. **Outward:** Congregation members volunteer together at a local food pantry or homeless shelter.
December 29	**Ujamaa** (Cooperative Economics)	**Inward:** Congregation holds a fundraiser to establish or increase the size of an emergency fund for members in need. **Outward:** Congregation identifies social justice and community organizations that it commits to supporting with a special collection during worship in the coming year.
December 30	**Nia** (Purpose)	**Inward:** Congregation examines its policies and systems through an antiracist, anti-oppressive, multicultural lens. **Outward:** Congregation partners with a reproductive rights organization to advocate for abortion rights.
December 31	**Kuumba** (Creativity)	**Inward:** Congregation holds a member talent show as part of its Watch Night observance (see Freedom Watch). **Outward:** Congregation establishes a college scholarship for performing arts students at a predominantly Black public high school.

January 1	**Imani** (Faith)	**Inward:** Congregation holds a January 1 worship service that celebrates African American contributions to Unitarian Universalism. **Outward:** Congregation holds a January 1 worship service that highlights the African American organizations and business it will support or partner with for the coming year.

In addition to activities consistent with the principle of the day, each evening people gather separately in their homes or collectively in their congregational or community settings to light the Kwanzaa candles. The following litany explains the principles and highlights the symbolism imbedded in the Kwanzaa table. Participants may take turns through the week leading the litany. The litany grows longer each night as more candles are lit and more principles are celebrated. Swahili words for the objects on the Kwanzaa table may be used instead of the English words.

Introduction

Call (Nights 1–7)**:** We gather at the end of every year to celebrate Kwanzaa.

Response (Nights 1–7)**:** A festival for the fruits of the year.

Call (Nights 1–7)**:** The straw mat (mkeka) represents tradition.

Response (Nights 1–7)**:** Upon tradition all else rests.

Call (Nights 1–7)**:** The ears of corn (muhinde) collectively represent our children.

Response (Nights 1–7)**:** Children are the hope of family, congregation, community, nation, and world.

Call (Nights 1–7)**:** The bowl of fruit and vegetables (bakuli la matunda na mboga) remind us of all we have to celebrate.

Response (Nights 1–7)**:** A harvest of success from the year just passed.

Call (Nights 1–7)**:** The candelabrum (kinara) holds the values we honor this season.

Response (Nights 1–7)**:** May they manifest in us now and throughout the year.

Call (Nights 1–7)**:** We light the seven candles (mishumaa saba) this season.

Response (Nights 1–7)**:** So that their flame will energize us all year long.

Candle Lighting

Light candles during the Call, going from left to right.

Call (Nights 1–7)**:** Umoja is unity.

Response (Nights 1–7)**:** We light this candle for the unity that binds us to one another.

Call (Nights 2–7)**:** Kujichagulia is self-determination.

Response (Nights 2–7)**:** We light a candle affirming our right to define and control our own lives.

Call (Nights 3–7)**:** Ujima is responsibility.

Response (Nights 3–7)**:** We light a candle reminding us that we are mutually accountable and have a duty to honor, respect, and aid one another.

Call (Nights 4–7)**:** Ujamaa is cooperative economics.

Response (Nights 4–7)**:** We light a candle reminding us of the prosperity that comes from working together.

Call (Nights 5–7)**:** Nia is purpose.

Response (Nights 5–7)**:** We light a candle for our strength of purpose and the courage of our conviction.

Call (Nights 6–7)**:** Kuumba is creativity.

Response (Nights 6–7)**:** We light a candle for the spirit that compels us to leave the world better than we inherited it.

Call (Night 7)**:** Imani is faith.

Response (Night 7)**:** We light a candle for our belief in ourselves, in one another, and in the collective spirit of which we are a part.

Closing

Call (Nights 1–7)**:** May these principles guide us this season and all year long.

Response (Nights 1–7)**:** Harambee! (translation: "Let's pull together").

Following the litany, the oldest takes a sip from the unity cup and passes it to the next oldest person, who does likewise until everyone has had a sip. After each sip, everyone exclaims *Ashé!* Gifts are exchanged the final day of Kwanzaa. In community settings, the evening may continue with African or African American-inspired entertainment, storytelling, movies, art exhibits featuring Black artists, Black fashion shows, or lectures and discussions on topics of significance in Black communities. As already noted, December 31 culminates in a Kwanzaa Karamu (see Karamu ritual) featuring cuisine from the African Diaspora.

Variations

Kwanzaa may be celebrated in addition to other end-of-the-year holidays typically recognized within UU congregations. This includes Christmas, Hannukah, and the winter solstice. Some congregations will recognize multiple holidays within a single worship service. Not everyone will be able to participate in the entire seven-day Kwanzaa holiday. Employment or other obligations may limit participation to a single or few days. This should not discourage you from participating in the parts of the holiday that you can, even if it is only an evening candle lighting.

Many Kwanzaa celebrations in the community occur on a single day, with families continuing the other days on their own. In these instances, the entire litany may be read followed by a Kwanzaa Karamu, regardless of which day it is. In some variations, candles are lit beginning with the center black candle and then alternating between the red and black candles, starting closest to the center and moving outward. Enliven the litany by encouraging an emotionally evocative call-and-response, especially at the end when the assembly exclaims *Harambee* and *Ashé!* Finally, try to include children and youth in all parts of the ritual and celebration.

In family celebrations, participants may be comfortable drinking from the unity cup. This should be avoided in community or congregational observances. In these instances, only the leader might drink while everyone exclaims *Ashé!* Alternatively, everyone may have a small cup of the beverage and drink together before closing with *Ashé!*

While gifts are traditionally given within families on the final day, households may try alternatives, including giving gifts the first day of Kwanzaa so that they can be enjoyed throughout the holiday. Another option is to give a small gift on each day of Kwanzaa.

Questions for Discussion

- What do each of the seven principles of Kwanzaa mean to you?
- What did you do in connection with each principle this year?
- What will you do in connection with each principle throughout the year?
- Is Kwanzaa a celebration only for Black people?
- How and when is it appropriate for other people to participate in Kwanzaa?
- How does your congregation handle Christian, Jewish, or other holiday celebrations, and how does or should this differ from the way the congregation participates in Kwanzaa?
- What does it mean for your congregation to participate in a holiday that began as part of the Black Nationalist Movement?
- Is Kwanzaa becoming commercialized like other December holidays? If so, what can you do about this?

Maafa

Purpose

To promote awareness of and healing from the horror of the Transatlantic slave trade.

Historical Inspiration

Dr. Marimba Ani, anthropologist and professor of African Studies at Hunter College, introduced the term *Maafa*—a Kiswahili word, pronounced *mah-AH-fah*, that translates to "great disaster"—to refer to the tragic effects of the Transatlantic Slave Trade.[24] The term "African Holocaust" is sometimes substituted for Maafa, although some object to using a word that has long been associated with the genocide of Jewish people during World War II.

Pastor Johnny Youngblood of St. Paul Community Baptist Church created the first Maafa commemoration in 1995. The St. Paul congregation continues this tradition nearly three decades later and is joined by religious, governmental, and community organizations throughout the United States and in Africa. These observances vary tremendously in content and often incorporate music, dance, poetry, plays, and prayer. They are particularly powerful when they involve coordinated observances at locations in Africa and the African Diaspora. Maafa

24 Marimba Ani, *Let the Circle Be Unbroken: The Implications of African Spirituality in the Diaspora* (Nkonimfo Publications, 1980).

ceremonies emphasize that although formal enslavement has ended, its effects continue in the systemic racism within societies today. Hence, the Maafa ritual is not only a commemoration of historical events but also a time to reflect upon the legacy of enslavement and to heal from historical and contemporary assaults on the dignity and value of Black lives.

Occasion and Frequency

Originally observed annually in the third week of September, Maafa ceremonies also take place on Juneteenth (see Freedom Watch) and other anniversaries of important events in the history of the enslavement of African people.

Setting

Maafa is a congregational or community-based commemoration.

Materials

This Maafa commemoration requires participants to wear white, a color sometimes associated with grief and mourning in Africa and the African Diaspora. Each participant will also receive a white or red flower. The white flowers commemorate tragic events during enslavement and the red flowers commemorate events in which lives were lost.

After flowers have been cast away, each participant should receive a small, handheld chalice in recognition of victories in the battle against racism and racial oppression. Participants also don a colorful stole, with a kente or other African fabric pattern, over their white mourning clothes.

For the music, participants may require printed lyrics of the freedom songs sung in the second half. African drums (such as djembe and dunun or djun djun drums) are also needed during the symbolic journey home of the spirits of those whose lives were lost during enslavement.

Ritual Preparation

Identify a procession route from your starting point to the body of water into which flowers will be cast. You may need to acquire permissions for use of the route and/or the body of water (see Variations for other options).

Choose which events will be remembered in the initial and return processions. These can be locally, nationally, or internationally recognized events, such as the passage of slavery laws and antislavery legislation, rebellions, and other civil rights milestones. UUs were involved in the abolitionist and civil rights movements, so events that highlight UU contributions and acknowledge UU complicity in enslavement are also appropriate choices.

Designate a few people to name these events as they hand out flowers and chalices. For a small group, the leader may be able to fulfill this role; for a larger one, multiple people may be advantageous. Identify other participants to play the drums. All others will participate as mourners by bringing flowers to the water and carrying chalices back.

The Ritual

Assembly and Invocation

As participants gather, each receives a red or white flower and is told which event the flower symbolizes. Once everyone is assembled, the ritual leader begins the invocation.

> On this day, we assemble to commemorate Maafa, the historical tragedy and the contemporary legacy of the enslavement

of African and African-descended people. We dress in white to mourn the loss of life and freedom. Each of you has been given an event to meditate on symbolized by the flower you hold—white for the many tragedies and red for the many lives lost as part of the painful legacy of enslavement. As we process in silence, I ask you to think about the event your flower symbolizes, the lives it impacted, and the legacy it leaves us today. We begin in silent mourning.

Procession to the Water

Participants move, as they are able, silently, respectfully, and solemnly to the body of water in which they will cast their flowers. The procession stops once the water is reached.

It took five weeks to cross the Atlantic chained in the hull of a slave ship. We pause now for five minutes, each minute representing a week of that horrific voyage. In the beat of the drum may we hear the laments of our enslaved ancestors.

Drums play softly for the next five minutes, then stop.

Casting of Flowers

As you walk forward to cast your flowers into the water, name aloud the event or loss it symbolizes.

Participants may cast flowers into the water singly or in groups. Continue when all flowers are cast:

Though the journey to enslavement took five weeks, throughout the Diaspora our people believed that after death their souls would return to Africa in a journey of nine days. Let the drums sound nine beats now to symbolize the journey home of all the souls lost to enslavement.

Drums play nine base beats spaced ten seconds apart.

Return Procession

Each participant receives a stole to don over the mourning clothes and a small chalice. As the chalice is lit, the participant is told a historical success in ending enslavement and overcoming oppression.

When all chalices are lit, the leader continues:

We came in remembrance, sorrow, and mourning; we return in mindfulness, strength, and determination. We return mindful of the legacy of enslavement in the world today, strengthened by our victories over oppression, and determined to overcome the challenges ahead. We came in silence; we return singing.

The procession returns singing the songs of freedom. Drums may accompany the singing. After the ritual is complete, the community celebrates with music and African dance performances, plays, or films that celebrate African heritage and the struggle for freedom.

Variations

While the ritual is particularly meaningful if flowers are cast into the Atlantic Ocean, geography may require other bodies of water to be used, including lakes, rivers, and ponds. Some participants may wish to commemorate events in their own family histories. In these instances, participants may bring their own red or white flowers to use in the ritual.

In traditional African mourning rituals, participants assemble by age. An alternative is to assemble by the length of time that has passed since each person's historical events have occurred.

With large groups, it may not be possible for everyone to participate in all parts of the ritual. Others may move with the participants, position themselves along the procession route, or gather at the water to witness the ritual. Candles, flashlights, or cell phone flashlight apps may be cheaper substitutes for chalices. Single flower petals may also be substituted for whole flowers. Similarly, paper sashes or individual items of African clothing brought by participants to wear for the return procession may be a cheaper alternative to stoles.

Questions for Discussion

- What events should be commemorated during the ritual and why?
- What is the legacy of enslavement today?
- What role did UUs play both in enslavement and in the abolition of slavery?
- What can we learn from the history of enslavement and from the role UUs played?
- What role is there for White UUs in the Maafa Ritual?
- What is the lasting impact of the Transatlantic Slave Trade for the descendants of the enslaved and the enslavers?
- What does the Transatlantic Slave Trade have to teach us about contemporary human trafficking?

Meditation/Spiritual Possession

Purpose

To achieve an alteration in everyday consciousness that relieves feelings of tension, stress, and disconnection and promotes feelings of joy, oneness, and transcendence.

Historical Inspiration

African theologian John S. Mbiti notes that spiritual possession in some form is ubiquitous across traditional African societies.[25] During possession, the individual personality becomes subordinate to a spiritual identity that may speak through the person to deliver knowledge and insights. The person may become capable of acts that they would not normally be able to perform. They may leap and dance in an uninhibited manner for hours with little apparent fatigue. At the end of the possession, the person may have no recollection of what occurred but may be left with a sense of joy and ecstasy.

Captured and enslaved Africans brought such traditions with them wherever they were taken. These traditions became a part of such African Diaspora religions as Santeria. They also found a place in Christianity, emerging in or influencing practices of Holy Spirit possession in the Pentecostal and Assemblies of God churches. When possessed by the Holy Spirit, these Christian believers enter an ecstatic

25 John S. Mbiti, *African Religions and Philosophy* (Anchor Books, 1970).

trance, speak a mostly unintelligible glossolalia, and feel as if they are in direct communication with a spiritual power. The Christian charismatic revival of the 1860s and 1870s spread these practices beyond the Pentecostal denomination so that a broader range of Christians began praying to the Holy Spirit for guidance, from which they received knowledge, healing, prophesy, and feelings of euphoria. In Spiritualist churches, sermons may be delivered by people believed to be possessed by spirits of the dead. The similarity to Mbiti's description of African spiritual possession is evident.

To those not accustomed to witnessing religious possession experiences, it may appear alarming or indicative of psychosis. Western psychiatrists studying possession at times associate it with clinical disorders such as depression, anxiety, psychosis, and epilepsy.[26] In contrast, anthropologists emphasize the social and psychological benefits of possession while still highlighting potential social, moral, and financial risks to vulnerable individuals.[27] In healthy individuals, possession experiences increase naturally occurring brain chemicals associated with pain relief and feelings of euphoria.[28] Western negative biases toward such experiences are diminishing, and possession experiences within a cultural or religious context are not automatically attributed to mental disorder unless they lead to decline in the individual's functioning within society.[29] In our ritual incorporation of elements of the possession experience, we emphasize the importance of reflection

26 G. Onchev, "Heterogeneity of the possession experiences: A case study from Pemba," *European Journal of Psychiatry* 15 (2001).

27 A. Masquelier, "From hostage to host: Confessions of a spirit medium in Niger," *Ethos* 30 (2002).

28 N. Kawai et al., "Catecholamines and opioid peptides increase in plasma in humans during possession trances," *Neuroreport* 12 (2001).

29 *Diagnostic and Statistical Manual of Mental Disorders*, 5th ed. (American Psychiatric Association, 2022).

and consultation should uncomfortable thoughts and feelings emerge during this ritual.

In secular terms, spiritual possession is an alteration in consciousness characterized by a feeling of oneness with something larger and transcendent. This alteration in consciousness may be induced in a variety of ways, including the techniques we typically associate with the African Diaspora such as rhythmic drumming, repetitive dance, chanting, and prayer.

While ceremonial possession is typically a community affair, it is not always so. Possession may come during private times as well, particularly to those who are adept at the experience. During times of stress, pain, or intense challenge, a spiritual possession may occur that brings calm, relief, and the capacity to endure. Sheila Walker[30] conducted anthropological studies of spiritual possession in African and Afro-American communities. In one anecdote, Walker describes a person undergoing surgery with minimal anesthesia. The person begins to chant, purportedly becomes possessed, and is then able to endure the procedure with relative calm.

The French anthropologist Dominique Zahn, studying the mystical practices of the Ibo, Yoruba, Ewe, Fon, Ashanti, and other cultural groups, notes that one may be initiated into these spiritual practices in two distinct ways.[31] The first, which we have already been describing, Zahn terms *epispanic initiation.* It involves training to attract a deity or spirit for a ritualized, ecstatic spiritual experience. The second, which is rarely included in discussions of African-inspired spirituality, Zahn calls *allotactic initiation.* It is a more sustained and personal quest for

---

30 Sheila S. Walker, *Ceremonial Spirit Possession in Africa and Afro-America* (E.J. Brill, 1972).

31 Dominique Zahn, "Some Reflections on African Spirituality," in *African Spirituality: Forms, Meanings, and Expressions*, ed. Jacob K. Olupona (Crossroad Publishing, 2000).

transcendent experience, emphasizing the intellect and the acquisition of knowledge to close the gap between the human and the divine. Spiritual possession happens to the epispanic initiate as an ecstatic experience, while it is acquired by the allotactic initiate with knowledge. In this respect, the allotactic experience is closer to the contemplative, meditative techniques of Buddhism.

From a more atheistic perspective, any guidance we receive during meditation comes from within ourselves. Meditative practices allow us to quiet our minds long enough to hear our own thoughts. It moves into the background ideas that previously dominated our thinking, allowing new thoughts and perspectives to emerge. Whether through spiritual possession or other forms, meditation is a powerful way to gain perspective on our lives.

Occasion and Frequency

The following ritual may be performed alone as a daily meditation at any time of the day when one has ten to thirty minutes of quiet, uninterrupted time. It can also be performed in a congregational or community setting.

Setting and Materials

The meditation ritual described below uses an Ashanti stool. Often carved from a single block of wood, these intricately designed African stools have found their way into the homes of some African Americans as decorative art or furniture. The Ashanti people, however, employ stools as sacred objects. According to legend, the Ashanti King Osei Tutu received a sacred golden stool in the eighteenth century from God. The golden stool became a revered object, symbolic of the monarchy and the seat of the collective spirit of the Ashanti people. It is never sat upon, not even by a king. A stool owned by an individual is likewise traditionally considered to be the seat of their soul, and care is taken to make sure no one uses it other than its proper owner. They feature a base and seat connected by columns carved in a variety of shapes. Ashanti stools are hollow, and the center space is easily accessible from either side. In this ritual, symbols of ancestors are placed in the hollow center of the stool, which could include a photograph of the ancestor, a letter written by the ancestor, an inherited piece of jewelry, or even an urn with cremated remains.

If a carved stool is not affordable or available, any small, low table that can serve as an altar may substitute. Optimally, the altar will be permanently dedicated to the meditation and not used for other purposes. Additional materials to place on the carved stool or altar table include a candle and candle holder (or chalice), a cup or goblet of water, and a bowl to hold libations poured from the cup. Enough water should be available to pour a libation to each ancestor named, reserving a little for the final libation. Whenever possible, consider supporting African artists and artisans by using cups and bowls handcrafted from natural materials like wood or clay, rather than mass-produced plastic.

The ritual also calls for music played by African drum and mbira (also known as a kalimba). Gather the instruments, if they will be played live, or recordings and a sound system.

The *mbira*, or African thumb piano, consists of metal keys attached to a wooden board and resonator. Vibrations of the metal keys produce ethereal music. The *mbira dzavadzimu,* known as the "voice of the ancestors," has been played for centuries in some African societies and was brought to South American communities during the slave trade. The instrument has been incorporated in popular music by bands such as *Earth, Wind, and Fire.* Recordings of traditional mbira music performed by contemporary African musicians are also available.

Ritual Preparation

Identify one or more ancestors that will be called upon as part of the ritual. These can be familial ancestors with whom you experience a personal connection or more widely revered individuals who serve as communal ancestors. Research the ancestor through family records and stories or, in the case of community figures, through biographies and memoirs. Learn as much about them as possible so that you see and hear them clearly in your mind and have an intuitive sense of their thoughts, beliefs, and personalities. You should know enough about the ancestor to answer plausibly the question of how they would think, speak, or act in a particular situation.

The Ritual

The following instructions are for group settings.

Invocation

The leader lights the candle and invites the symbolic presence of the ancestors.

> Ancestral spirits, we invite you to this altar.

Lift the goblet to pour libations to the ancestors about to be named into the bowl.

> We pour this libation to honor our ancestors of African descent whose names have not been passed down to us. Slavery separates us from a part of our past. There will always be more ancestors unknown to us than are known. With this libation, we pay respect to the ancestors we can never know but whose courage and endurance made our lives possible.

Raise the goblet high.

With these libations we honor our ancestors known to us by name. I invite you to speak the names of your ancestors.

With each ancestor named, pour a libation. Stop pouring before the goblet is emptied to reserve water for the final libation. Ancestors that do not receive an individual libation are collectively honored with the final libation.

With this final libation, we honor you all.

Replace the goblet.

Ancestral spirits, we thank you for your presence at our altar and for your many blessings in our lives. We thank you not only for past blessings but also for the ways you continue to bless us through the rich and powerful memories that possess, guide, and empower us.

Induction

Lower or turn off lights so that the candle flame provides the main illumination. Began softly and slowly playing African drum music.

Eyes open or closed as each of us desires, let the drum rhythm lead us into a deeper connection with the spirits of our ancestors. As the rhythm moves you, tap your feet, clap your hands, nod your head, sway your body, or get up and dance. Let the rhythm guide us to the ancestors.

Music can be live or recorded but should begin softly so that the leader remains audible, but then grow in volume so that only the drumming is heard. The rhythm should be repetitive, with few changes in pattern, though the intensity can grow by increasing volume and pacing. The music can last five to fifteen minutes, as chosen by the ritual leader.

At the end of this period, the rhythm should slow and grow quieter until its pace is back to where it started.

> As the spirits move you, settle into your sitting position and breathe to the rhythm.

Continue the soft drumming for another one to two minutes, then fade.

Chanting

The room should now be silent save for the sound of breathing.

> Breathe in together and say silently to yourself: Ancestral spirits live within me.

> Pause for inhalation and silent chant.

> Breathe out together and say silently: Ancestral spirits possess and guide me.

Repeat these instructions until all are inhaling and exhaling together in synchrony with the silent chants. The leader may exaggerate their own breath sounds to help set the pace. Breathing should be slow and deep, completely filling the lungs upon inhalation and completely emptying them with each exhalation. It may take some time to achieve this, depending upon how physically active participants were during the drumming.

Continue breathing and silent chanting for five to fifteen minutes, then draw the chanting to a close.

> One final time together. Breathe in as you silently say: Ancestral spirits live within me. Now breathe out, as you silently say: Ancestral spirits possess and guide me. Now let your mind grow still as you continue to breathe.

Mindfulness

After a minute of silence, the leader says:

> We carry our ancestors within us in the stories we've heard and the personal memories we've formed. Let them speak to us now. Let them speak to what troubles our minds and relieve what burdens our hearts. Ancestral spirits bring us guidance and bring us joy.
>
> Personal experience of an ancestor is powerful, but not essential. Nor is it essential that it be our personal ancestor. It may be an ancestor we have borrowed—any person who has moved, motivated, and impacted us deeply. What is essential is the depth of connection we feel with the memories of that person. What is essential is the richness of knowledge we have acquired and assimilated into our mental model of this ancestor.

Continue to sit in mindful silence for five to ten minutes, with the leader repeating two or three times during this period:

> Ancestral spirits bring us guidance and bring us joy.

Closing

Begin playing soft mbira music, live or recorded. After about one minute of music, the leader says:

> Let the music draw us back to the present moment. Let the music bring us back to the external world. Let us bring the joy of the spirit with us. Let us bring the guidance of the ancestors into our lives. As we open our eyes, let us see with a new vision and enter life with a new wisdom.

Let the music play for one to two minutes as the lights come up. When it stops, close with:

> Ancestral spirits, as you depart our altar, may we always love, honor, remember, and revere you. May we be guided and moved by the spirits within. Ashé.

Extinguish the candle and later return to nature the water poured in libation. Allow people to stretch and move around, before sitting again.

Sharing

Invite participants to share what they felt and learned during the session. Some people with psychological or psychiatric conditions are drawn to meditative and other spiritual practices, and the ideas that emerge can be troubling or painful. Sharing the feelings and insights gained during this meditative practice gives a community an opportunity to detect signs of a mental health crisis that may require professional intervention. Even if practicing the ritual alone, it is advisable to later check out the insights gained with other people.

If desired, end the session with a shared meal.

Variations

The language and format of the ritual may be adapted for individual or community practice. The full ritual may be too long for daily practice. Consider selecting the parts of the ritual that are particularly helpful to you for more regular practice.

Questions for Discussion

- What role does meditation play in my life?
- This ritual includes elements of both ecstatic and contemplative meditation. How well do each of these approaches to meditation work for me, and why?
- How often do I want to practice this or other meditation rituals? How can I find time for rituals like this in my busy life?
- What does it mean to carry my ancestors with me in my memory or knowledge of them?
- Do I see my ancestors as spiritual beings separate from my own consciousness, or do I believe they exist only in memory? In what ways do these beliefs shape how I approach this ritual?
- What parts of this ritual brought me joy?
- What, if any, uncomfortable thoughts or feelings emerged during this ritual? With whom can I share these uncomfortable thoughts or feelings?
- What new insights arose during this ritual? How do I wish these insights to become manifest in my daily life?

Prayer

Purpose

To bring awareness of human need and emotion to that which is experienced as transcendent and divine.

Historical Inspiration

Within African traditional religion, to engage in prayer is to be "in communion with divine reality."[32] Consistent with Unitarian Universalism, divine reality is experienced and understood within African traditions in innumerable ways. Ethnic groups vary in the degree to which divinity is understood in anthropomorphic terms, such as a grandfather to the people, or as an abstract ideal, such as the supreme manifestation of life itself. In some African-derived cultures, God is seen as remote and distant from human affairs. Many people pray to intermediaries, including minor deities, spirits that manifest themselves in nature, and ancestral figures, given their more intimate and immediate relationship with the person praying. Prayer, therefore, is not limited to a particular understanding of divine reality and may be addressed to an abstract conception of the divine or to closer and more intimate personifications of the divine within one's life.

32 Aylward Shorter, "Prayer in the Religious Traditions of Africa, I," *The Way* 23, no. 1 (January 1983), https://www.theway.org.uk/back/23Shorter.pdf.

Given the existential pain of colonialism and slavery, prayers across the African Diaspora are often petitionary—a request for deliverance from the harsh and grim realities of an imposed subservience to the will, whims, and needs of others. Such petitions can be heartrending and uniquely eloquent in their call for liberation. Yet the full range of human need is reflected in prayers of people of African descent collected across the centuries.[33] These "conversations with God" are full of hope, love, gratitude, regret, blessing, reverence, introspection, zeal, and more. In forming prayer, one need only ask: How do I understand and address the divine, and what is moving me to pray in this moment? The answer to these questions is your prayer.

Belief in the power of prayer is held strongly throughout the African Diaspora, a power often brought to bear when someone is facing illness or crisis. Ultimately prayers are words, and their power lies in the impact of the words themselves. Janheinz Jahn, the scholar of the Negritude cultural movement, captured this power in the concept of *nommo,* a Bantu word referring to a fluidic mixture of water and heat that issues from the mouth when words are spoken.[34] More symbolically, nommo embodies the creative power attributed to words spoken in prayer, incantation, curse, or blessing.

Occasion and Frequency

Prayer may be as frequent as human need requires and may occur privately or within families or communities. When praying within family or community, care must be taken to clearly state that you are praying based on your personal theological understanding of the

33 James Melvin Washington, *Conversations with God: Two Centuries of Prayers by African Americans* (HarperCollins, 1994).

34 Janheinz Jahn, *Muntu: African Culture and the Western World*, trans. Marjorie Grene (Grove Press, 1961).

divine, which may differ from the understanding others hold. Optimally, however, families and communities will develop a common and acceptable language that does not exclude anyone from full and deep participation in the ritual. Similarly, the word or phrase used to close a prayer should be chosen with the same care and respect used to address the divine. Besides the traditional *Amen* used in Christian prayers or *Ameen* used in Islam, *Ashé* is increasingly used in the African Diaspora.

Setting

Within African traditional cultures, all aspects of public and private life are touched by the religion that is universally shared within the culture. In a pluralistic, multicultural society that embraces separation of church and state, prayer is not always appropriate outside of the home or congregation, unless it is done privately or utilizes sufficiently open language that respects and allows for individual interpretation. Before initiating such prayers, consider how they will land for others in a shared space.

Materials

Prayer requires no material other than a means of expression. If one understands prayer as a petition to a wish-granting, bargain-making personal deity, then the cost is disappointment when the prayer goes unfulfilled. As we mature in our relationship with the divine, we become less likely to ask for a specific and measurable outcome. The great benefit of prayer within families is the opportunity it provides for parents to model mature prayer and to help children transition from material petitions to more spiritual conversations with the divine.

Ritual Preparation

Consider the people who are about to hear the prayer and whether the language chosen will aid or impede them receiving the intended benefit. Choose words that will allow each person to call forth the divine. If the right words are unknown, invite the participants to speak for themselves the words that best represent the divine. Also, consider the need that is being addressed in the prayer and whether it is worthy of invoking what you hold most sacred. If there is a petition or plea included in the prayer, it should be one that is within the power of words to deliver.

The Ritual

Though each prayer will be unique, the following general template may be used:

1. Calling to the Divine
2. Naming Your Motive
3. Expressing Your Hopes
4. Closing with an Affirmation

Variations

Prayer is for individuals, congregations, and communities, and its variety is infinite. Here are just a few examples. The numbers in brackets correspond to the above template.

Individual Prayer for Forgiveness

> [1] Spirit of love and forgiveness, [2] I know I have caused pain and hurt to the one whom I love. [3] May they see in my

behavior how deeply sorry I am and how sincere my commitment is to earn their trust and faith again. May I earn their forgiveness and may I continue to know their love. [4] Ashé.

Family Prayer for Thanks

[1] Spirit of nature, [2] we are grateful for the bounty that sustains our lives and allows us to thrive. [3] May we always remember to be grateful, even in the most difficult and challenging times, for the bounty and grace surrounding our family. [4] Ashé.

Community Prayer for Strength

[1] We call into this present moment of grief the spirits of our ancestors. I invite you to say their names, calling them into this space. Those whose survival yesterday of the worst a human being could face make our own lives possible today. Those whose courage and strength inspire us even now in this time of grief and loss. [2] Too many of our young have died at the hands of injustice. Too many mothers, fathers, siblings, friends, neighbors, and loved ones have cried tears of pain and loss, almost to the point of hopelessness. [3] Yet, ancestors, in your example of unflinching courage, unrelenting belief, and unceasing struggle, may we find courage stoked, belief renewed, strength restored, and hope eternal. May your example be with us, inspiring us to keep seeking that better day. To struggle on one more day, and then the day after, and the day after that. [4] May our words prayed in earnestness and faith make this so. Ashé.

Questions for Discussion

- What names do we use for the holy or divine?
- What do these names communicate about our theology?
- What names for the holy or divine interfere with our ability to engage in prayer, and why?
- How does it feel to be part of a family or community that possesses diverse conceptions of the divine?
- What motivates you to pray?
- What do you expect to gain, receive, or accomplish through prayer? How have these expectations changed over the course of your life?
- What does it mean for a prayer to have been answered?

Transcendent Spirit

Purpose

To experience a spiritual sacredness within nature.

Historical Inspiration

Traditional African religions variously describe their deities in highly anthropomorphic or highly abstract terms. Perhaps the least anthropomorphic deity is the Ibo conception of God, *Chukwu.* The root of this word is "chi," meaning "life" in the Ibo language. The Ibo believe that a part of Chukwu exists in all things. Animate life, including humankind, is distinguished from the inanimate world by its greater apportionment of chi. Janheinz Jahn, in his classic book on Bantu culture and the Western world, calls this force *ntu.*[35] The Mende people call it *ndevui,* and the Yoruba call it *ori.* Regardless of the language, what is being described is a primal force within nature from which all living existence flows. The African spirit is immanent in nature and has no existence outside of the natural, material world. In this sense, African-inspired spirituality is fundamentally about the enchantment of nature.

Belief in an inspirited nature demands a reverential rather than an exploitive approach to our universe and the life it creates. It similarly demands a reverence from each human being as a bearer of this same

35 Jahn, *Muntu.*

sacred force. Nature becomes a source of inspiration and transcendence. African-centered spiritual traditions share with Unitarian Transcendentalism this reverence for the spiritual qualities of nature. Ecstatic rituals (see Meditation/Spiritual Possession) within African-derived spiritual traditions aim to bring about a deeper understanding and engagement with this spiritual essence. Perceiving it inspires a range of emotions, a subset of which are captured in the litany.

Occasion and Frequency

Participate in the ritual as often as needed or desired to remind oneself of the natural spirit surrounding us.

Setting

This ritual may be practiced in any environment in which contact with nature is possible. A mountain, a body of water, a patch of sky, a plant on a windowsill, or even stones placed upon a table will all suffice.

We perceive nature as beautiful whether we view it on the microscopic or the macroscopic scale. Even in the most ravaged environment, the spiritual essence of nature and the beauty within it will be available somewhere, seemingly waiting to be noticed.

Ritual Preparation

No preparation is necessary beyond finding a natural setting in which to practice the ritual.

The Ritual

Go into nature with no expectation. Accept whatever happens with gratitude, but also take care. Nature's harsher realities are present even when you are admiring it. Nature bites, stings, and burns even while it inspires our awe.

Take a few minutes to experience nature with as many senses as the setting will allow. Appreciate the depth of beauty within nature. Breathe in deeply and try to encounter the environment with each of your senses. See nature, listen to its sounds, smell its odor, feel the impression it makes on your skin.

When you are fully present, recite from memory (or read) the provided litany, pausing after each sentence to appreciate the meaning of the words. When completed, rest in this natural setting as long as you desire, remaining aware of how nature is stimulating each of your senses. Upon occasion, you may find yourself moved to tears, to laughter, or both. As you focus on each of your senses, you may even find that you lose yourself and experience a sense of oneness with the part of nature that has captured your attention. Recite the litany a second time just before you leave.

Call: There is a spirit within nature,

Response: And a spirit within me.

Call: Perceiving Its presence,

Response: I am filled with joy, and I strive to be mindful.

Call: Perceiving Its grandeur,

Response: I am filled with reverence, and I approach to worship.

Call: Perceiving Its power,

Response: I am filled with humbleness, and I strive to be in harmony.

Call: Perceiving Its beneficence,

Response: I am filled with gratitude, and I am moved to serve others.

Call: Perceiving Its mystery,

Response: I am filled with wonder, and the passion to discover.

Call: This then is the Spirit within nature,

Response: And the nature of the Spirit within me. Ashé.[36]

Variations

If alone, recite both the call and response. If in a group, one person may lead with the call while the rest respond, or the group can divide evenly into halves, each reciting the call or response to the other. All should say *Ashé* at the end.

Questions for Discussion

- Have you ever experienced a sense of sacredness in the natural world? If so, when and how did this occur?
- Have you ever experienced a sense of oneness with the sacred in nature? If so, what was this experience like?
- What thoughts and feelings did it prompt?
- How does this perception of the sacred in nature affect the way you live in the world?
- Discriminatory housing and lending practices leave many African Americans living in communities that are in proximity to sources of environmental pollution and that have little direct access to green space. What are the spiritual consequences of this form of systemic racism?

36 Anthony Y. Stringer, "African Spirit," in *BLUU Notes: An Anthology of Love, Justice, and Liberation*, ed. Takiyah Nur Amin and Mykal Slack (Skinner House Books, 2021).

True Spirit

Purpose

To affirm Black LGBTQI+ identity, here referred to as "true spirit."

Historical Inspiration

As of this writing, same-sex relationships are subject to criminal prosecution in thirty-two African countries, in four of which it is punishable by death.[37] Despite this, there is considerable evidence for precolonial acceptance of same-sex relationships, gender nonconformity, and nonbinary gender behavior across sub-Saharan Africa.[38]

This evidence includes early European explorer accounts of gender nonconformity in traditional tribal dress. In addition, multiple

37 "LGBTQ in Africa: Statistics and Facts," Statista, accessed June 21, 2022, https://www.statista.com/topics/8602/lgbtq-in-africa/#dossierContents__outerWrapper.

38 *Nonbinary gender:* Zeynep Sasmazel, "Gender Expression and Sexual Identity in African Cultures Existed Outside the Binary Until Imperialism," *Hornet*, October 18, 2021, https://hornet.com/stories/lgbtq-african-cultures/.

Same-sex relationships: Bernardine Evaristo, "The idea that African Homosexuality was a Colonial Import is a Myth," *The Guardian*, March 8, 2014, https://www.theguardian.com/commentisfree/2014/mar/08/african-homosexuality-colonial-import-myth.

Precolonial acceptance: Sexual Minorities Uganda, *Expanded Criminalisation of Homosexuality in Uganda: A Flawed Narrative*, January 2014, https://caladvocacyblog.files.wordpress.com/2014/01/expanded-criminalisation-of-homosexuality-in-uganda-january-2014.pdf.

indigenous African languages include words for what today we call queer identity. Ethnic groups in Angola, Burundi, Nigeria, Rwanda, Sudan, and elsewhere incorporate same-sex practices in spiritual rituals. In common with peoples and cultures throughout the world, ethnic groups in Cameroon and Gabon engaged in same-sex intercourse and the Nzima of Ghana permitted same-sex marriage well in advance of the European subjugation and colonization of Africa. The current antipathy to these practices owes much to the influence of colonization and religious conversion.

Similarly, in the African Diaspora, fundamentalist religious affiliation tends to be associated with negative views of same-sex marriage and nonconformity to traditional gender expectations. This appears to be changing, though, in people identifying as Black Protestants.[39] Unitarian Universalism openly welcomes LGBTQI+ participation in its ministry and religious community and attempts to dismantle stereotypes and build self-acceptance and self-esteem across the lifespan through the *Our Whole Lives* sexuality education curricula. Such openness has made the UU denomination a destination and haven for many LGBTQI+ African Americans who face rejection even in Black family and community spaces. The following coming-out ritual grounds the discovery and celebration of "true spirit" in the precolonial African heritage that acknowledged and engaged with the full range of sexual and gender identities.

Occasion and Frequency

Typically, this ritual would be performed once in a person's lifetime. Gender and sexual identity may evolve and unfold in different ways over a lifespan, creating the possibility for a repeat of this ritual at later times.

39 B. Cooper et al., *PRRI August 2016 LGBT Survey*, May 27, 2022, https://www.thearda.com/data-archive?fid=PRRI0816.

Setting

This ritual is intended for home, congregational, or other community settings.

Materials

This ritual requires a chalice and a combustible object that represents the self that is being left for the self you are becoming or have become.

Ritual Preparation

The participant in the ritual will need to craft a message to the identity that is being left behind. This message should express all the feelings associated with the former identity. This former identity may be addressed by name, particularly if a new name is used going forward. There are likely to be a multitude of emotions—such as anger, joy, gratitude, and sadness—felt about the previous identity. Craft a parting message that brings closure, that says what needs to be said in order to be able to move on to the new identity.

Provide the ritual leader with a combustible token of the former self that will be consumed in the lit chalice during this ritual. This can be a photo of the former self, a piece of paper with the former name written on it, or another symbol with meaning to the participant.

Finally, identify people who can offer a brief welcome after the coming-out. These should be personal statements expressing each person's unique observations, thoughts, and emotions. The tone of statements does not have to be serious. They can contain humorous or moving anecdotes that capture a core message or reaction. All should include a welcome to or a blessing of the person coming out.

The Ritual

The leader begins with a chalice lighting and reading selected to reflect the identity being affirmed.

Leader: [Name] (use person's preferred name) and Dear Ones, we come together to recognize, affirm, welcome, and celebrate [Name]'s coming-out as [identity]. We recognize that all that has happened in [Name]'s life before has led to who [they] are now. Some of this may have been painful. Some of this may have been joyful. But all of it is a part of what makes you who you are. [Name], I give you this time to say a message of thanks, regret, anger, sadness, joy, gratitude, or whatever else you wish to say as you bid farewell to the you that is ending.

Participant: Read or recite your farewell message to the former you.

Leader: [Name], you have given me this token of your former self, which I place now in the chalice to ignite and burn, symbolic of your leaving your past self for the new self you have become.

Participant: I say goodbye, knowing that parts of you will remain a part of me, as I go on.

Leader: Now I invite you to introduce or, as the case may be, to reintroduce the true self that is officially coming out today.

Participant: Read or recite your description of the true self that is coming out. Begin with the words: I would like to introduce my true self. This is who I am (alternative: This is who I am becoming). This statement may include a name if the participant is taking a new one.

Leader: Before we were colonized or enslaved, we honored true spirit. This fact has been hidden in history's closet, but it too is coming out today. As I call out who we are and have always been, I ask that you respond with "We honor true spirit." Say it now.

Community: We honor true spirit.

Leader: From the female warriors of ancient Dahomey to the male grandmothers of ancient Congo, we honor gender diversity and gender fluidity in the free and uncolonized people of Africa.

Community: We honor true spirit.

Leader: From the seventeenth-century warrior that history calls Queen Nzinga, who dressed in the male garb of her people, ruled as their king, and had a harem of men who dressed as wives to the openly gay nineteenth-century King Mwango the Second of the Baganda people, we honor true spirit.

Community: We honor true spirit.

Leader: From the Nandi and Kisii women of Kenya, the Ibo women of Nigeria, the Nuer women of Sudan, the Kuria women of Tanzania to the Nilotico Lango men of Uganda and the Azande warriors of Northern Congo, we honor women marrying women and men marrying men in free and uncolonized Africa.

Community: We honor true spirit.

Leader: From the male farmers of Cameroon and Gabon for whom sex with men was a medicine to the female seers of the African Cape for whom sex with women prepared them for divination, we honor the power that flows from true spirit.

Community: We honor true spirit.

Leader: I invite those of you who [Name] has chosen to come forward now to say a word of welcome to the person coming out today.

Family, friends, mentors, etc. who were previously chosen should now come forward to read or recite their welcome messages. Each statement should end with a hug, handshake, or other gesture of welcome. Once all are completed, the Leader closes the ritual.

Leader: If there are no more statements, [Name], I too want to add my welcome and want to give you this blessing. At this time when your body is joining your soul, when your life is becoming one with your spirit, know that your journey is just beginning. There is more to unfold. The journey will not always be easy, but you are not on this journey alone. We journey with you. When you are turned away, turn to us. When you face anger, we will give you love. When you face conflict, come to us for peace. When you are tired, find your rest in our arms. When you feel doubt, find reassurance in our eyes. When you are hated for being what you are, turn to us for love. We love you. The you that you are today. The you that you will become tomorrow. What has begun today in love will continue tomorrow in love, and so may it be through all time. Ashé.

Variations

This ritual is a collaboration between the person coming out and one or more ritual leaders, who may be relatives, friends, mentors, ministers, etc. The above ritual assumes one leader, but this role can be divided between multiple people as needed. The welcome statement can be varied to include any meaningful form of expression, including a poem, song, piece of music, and so on. The important factor is that they communicate a personal message that acknowledges and welcomes the person coming out. Care must be taken to not allow this to become a time for negative or unkind messages from family or others who do not truly welcome the participant's coming-out. Invitations should only include those who will be supportive and welcoming, and the ritual leader must be prepared to intervene should anyone attempt to subvert the intent of the ritual.

Questions for Discussion

- Which parts of my previous identity do I carry with me?
- Which parts of my previous identity do I leave?
- For what in my previous life or identity am I grateful, joyful, and thankful?
- How does it affect me to know there is a long tradition of acceptance and welcome of LGBTQI+ identities in Africa that, in many instances, contrasts with contemporary attitudes?
- What is the connection between negative attitudes toward people with LGBTQI+ identity in African Diaspora communities and exposure to fundamentalist ideas that were not a part of precolonial and pre-enslavement Africa?

Ubuntu

Purpose

To link individual achievement with community achievement.

Historical Inspiration

Ubuntu is an African philosophical concept summarized by such phrases as "I am because we are," and "A person is a person through other people."[40] They demonstrate the idea that a human being cannot exist in a vacuum. Everyone is tied to a larger community and only attains humanity in relationship to the larger collective. The concept has been a part of African culture into antiquity, but its modern usage began in association with liberation from colonialism in Zimbabwe and from apartheid in South Africa. The late South African spiritual leader and activist Archbishop Desmond Tutu's articulation of the concept helped it spread throughout the African Diaspora.

Ubuntu embodies a uniquely African humanism and is part of the effort to correct both the injustice of colonization and excessive focus on individualism that colonizers brought to Africa from their own cultures. For similar reasons, ubuntu has found fertile reception with those who perceive life in western societies as lonely and

40 Stanlake John Thompson Samkange and Tommie Marie Samkange, *Hunhuism or Ubuntuism: A Zimbabwe Indigenous Political Philosophy* (Graham Publishing, 1980).

isolating. In contrast, more collectivist societies are sometimes criticized as sacrificing the rights of individuals in favor of the needs of the group. Ubuntu emphasizes that the linkage between one and all is two-way. It affirms both the I and the We, putting them on equal footing and highlighting that neither can be neglected or sacrificed for the other.

This ritual reminds us of the connection between the individual and community. It is intended to symbolically link individual with collective achievement and success. It also includes a tangible connection between the two by requiring a "sacrifice" or pledge through which individual profit (material or otherwise) benefits the larger community, while the larger community supports the individual.

The Ubuntu ritual is like the Atonement and Forgiveness ritual in that it includes the sacrifice of a thing of value to the individual. In traditional societies, the animals you owned reflected your wealth. Sacrifices were made to bring spiritual favor upon oneself and the community. Hence, sacrificing an animal was offering a thing of both spiritual and material value in service to a higher good. Animal sacrifice continues to be a part of some African spiritual traditions but is considered cruel and unacceptable in most contemporary societies. The sacrifice included in the Ubuntu ritual is either monetary or an act of volunteer service, both of which are acceptable to Unitarian Universalists.

Occasion and Frequency

Consider engaging in this ritual at the start of a new endeavor that is anticipated to bring rewards that you wish to share with your larger community. That may be a job, an investment, a project, or similar. It may also be performed after you are experiencing rewards or profit from an endeavor that is already underway.

Setting

This ritual is intended for individuals or families to perform in their home.

Materials

This ritual requires a personal sacrifice, written or symbolized, in a form that can be placed upon a table or altar. The sacrifice can be ongoing (e.g., a recurring donation or a commitment to monthly volunteering) and should be proportional to your gain or achievement. The only other materials required are a chalice and an altar or table.

Ritual Preparation

Identify a charity or cause you wish to link to your achievement and success. Commit to a sacrifice of worth—time, wealth, or both—that is proportionate to your own return.

The Ritual

Place the sacrifice on a table or altar. Dim lights in the room, and light the chalice. After the chalice is lit, say the following litany, repeating each line twice before going to the next. Recite each line first with respect to yourself and the second time with respect to the larger community.

> With this sacrifice, I affirm that I am because we are.
> With this sacrifice, I affirm that we are because I am.
> With this sacrifice, I affirm my connection to others.
> With this sacrifice, I affirm the connection of others to me.
> With this sacrifice, I affirm the sacred spirit within myself.
> With this sacrifice, I affirm the sacred spirit within others.

With this sacrifice, I link myself to my community.
With this sacrifice, I link my community to myself.
With this sacrifice, I affirm that I am because we are.
With this sacrifice, I affirm that we are because I am.

As you extinguish the chalice, close the litany:

Ashé.

Keep the commitment to making the sacrifice.

Variations

A family may perform the ritual together if they are committing to a joint sacrifice to a cause they share. Congregations might encourage members to perform this ritual in association with their annual pledge, reminding members that making a pledge is an act reflecting the principle of ubuntu.

Questions for Discussion

- How do you support your community?
- How does your community support you?
- How should the needs of the individual and community be balanced?
- How can we practice ubuntu in an individualistic society?

Warriorship

Purpose

To gain strength and resilience in the face of personal challenge.

Historical Inspiration

Several African traditions embrace a type of reincarnation, though it differs from the more familiar Hindu and Buddhist conceptions. In these Eastern religions, a soul may travel through many bodies until it finds liberation from the cycle of birth and death. In the Yoruba, Akan, and Ibo traditions, reincarnation is much closer to modern ideas about heredity in which characteristics of one's ancestors are passed down to offspring.[41] At birth, relatives scrutinize an infant's features and behavior for signs of the ancestors in the newborn. Ancestral characteristics may be reincarnated while the ancestor remains alive and can simultaneously reside in living siblings.

The challenges people of African descent have faced throughout Africa and the African Diaspora reinforce a tradition of venerating not only ancestors but also great men and women who courageously

41 *Yoruba:* E. Bolaji Idowu, O*lodumare: God in Yoruba Belief* (Longmans, 1966).
Akan: Kwame Gyeke, "The Relation of *Ōkra* (Soul) and *Honam* (Body): An Akan Conception," in *African Philosophy: An Anthology*, ed. Emmanuel Chukwudi Eze (Blackwell, 1998).
Ibo: Chinua Achebe, "'Chi' in Igbo Cosmology," in *African Philosophy: An Anthology*, ed. Emmanuel Chukwudi Eze (Blackwell, 1998).

challenged, withstood, and overcame injustice and oppression. Even "ordinary" people, who did nothing more than what was necessary for the survival of themselves, their families, and their community, are venerated, though their accomplishments may be known to only a few. They all are a part of the inheritance, both biological and cultural, that makes us mighty. The Warrior ritual calls upon this heritage, reminding us of what makes us strong and motivating us to face whatever challenges life brings.

Occasion and Frequency

The Warrior ritual may be performed as often as needed to draw upon the strengths necessary to face a challenge.

Setting

This ritual is intended to be done at home.

Materials

Choose something that represents the person whose strengths and characteristics you wish to draw into yourself, such as a picture or other object. If possible, put these pictures in frames or otherwise prop them up so that they are vertically visible. These can be biological ancestors or cultural ones, who are not hereditarily related but whose characteristics you wish to find and instill within yourself. Place a candle in a candle holder adjacent to each picture or symbol of the person you will call upon. An altar or table is needed to hold the candles and pictures, with a few inches separating the representation of each person. Burning sticks of incense may be added to the altar or table if desired.

Ritual Preparation

Identify the challenge you are facing, and think of what within yourself may prevent you from facing and overcoming it. Consider the characteristics you will need to embody to overcome the challenge. They might be courage, intelligence, creativity, compassion, speaking ability, capacity for mercy, or even vulnerability—whatever is needed in your current circumstance. Be as specific as possible when naming them.

Consider who among your ancestors, both familial and cultural, best represents these desired characteristics. Be creative in the ancestral figures you identify; they do not have to be the obvious choices. Research each person whose strengths you wish to draw upon so that you can imagine how they would confront the challenge you face.

The chosen person does not need to be perfect to inspire you. They were human beings with faults and limitations who surely looked to others for inspiration, just as you now look to them.

The Ritual

> Warrior Spirit of my ancestors, be with me as I face [specify challenge].

Light the candle adjacent to the picture of the first ancestor. Speak the ancestor's name.

> [Name], may I have your [characteristic you wish to embody] as I face my challenge.

Fix your eyes on the image or symbol of the ancestor for a few seconds, then close your eyes as you imagine how they made use of the desired characteristic. With your inhalations, imagine this characteristic pouring into you and fully infusing your entire being. Hold your breath as it permeates you. On your exhalation, imagine it remaining a part of you while you expel whatever thoughts, emotions, or other personal limitations might impede you from fully embodying it.

Repeat this visualization with each inhalation and exhalation for several minutes. Continue until you feel empowered with the desired characteristic.

> [Name of ancestor], thank you for the gift of [desired characteristic].

Repeat with each of the ancestors and characteristics you have identified. After having meditated upon embodying the strengths of each ancestor, conclude with:

> Warrior spirit, fill me. Warrior spirit, make me [repeat the characteristics you now embody].

Pause to imagine how you will use this new strength in confronting your challenge.

> Ashé.

Variations

While primarily intended for individual practice, the ritual can be adapted for family or congregational use, particularly when a common challenge is being faced together. For congregations, identify public figures known to the entire community as the ancestors whose characteristics are needed in meeting the challenge. Alternately, ask congregants to identify a personal or public ancestor and to come forward to speak the person's name and tell a brief anecdote about the characteristics they possessed that will inspire the community as they imagine taking the characteristic into themselves.

Questions for Discussion

- What is the nature of the challenge you face?
- What fears or doubts are you experiencing?
- What similar challenges have you faced?
- What characteristics have gotten you through such challenges?
- What has caused you to fail in meeting similar challenges before?

Winds of Change

Purpose

To motivate and create acceptance of change.

Historical Inspiration

While rituals embody the values and traditions of a culture, they also play a role in social change.[42] African and African-inspired communities use ritual at moments when there is potential for disruption, such as during seasonal changes or in response to individual or collective crises.[43] Rituals strengthen community and individual alike, helping people cope with transition by providing familiar ways to encounter it.

This ritual draws inspiration from the African village tradition of sweeping the home each morning, both to preserve cleanliness and to eliminate any evil spiritual influences that may have accumulated overnight. African and African Diasporan spirituality is replete with nature deities. The Yoruba, for example, honor deities associated with thunder and lightning (Shango), air (Ayao), the earth (Ile), the sea and other waters (Olokun, Oya, Oshun, and Yewa), and others. These nature

42 Samuel Manaseh Yirenkyi, "Ritual Performative Ceremonies and Values in the African Context," *International Journal of African and Asian Studies* 57 (August 31, 2019), https://www.iiste.org/Journals/index.php/JAAS/article/view/49078.

43 A. K. Awedoba, *Culture and Development in Africa with Special Reference to Ghana* (Institute of African Studies, University of Ghana, 2002).

deities traveled west with enslaved Africans to become Santeria's Oya and Yemaya, the goddesses of wind and water, respectively. In keeping with these traditions, this ritual of change incorporates wind, fire, and water, all forces of nature with the power to alter the landscape.

Occasion and Frequency

The trigger for this ritual is typically the desire for or onset of a change in personal, congregational, or community life. It may be performed as frequently as needed. The ritual is best performed just before the dawn of a new day.

Setting

This ritual is appropriate for home, congregational, and community settings. The example to come focuses on the individual but can be modified for a congregation or other community.

Materials

This ritual requires four white candles in candle holders, a source of fire to light the candles, an African broom (often bristles bound together without a handle, similar to a Western whisk broom), four sheets of paper, a noncombustible bowl or pot, a bowl of water, a small table, and a cushion or low stool.

Ritual Preparation

Decide on the change you wish to see or the change you must accept. Define a circular ritual space by marking the directions of north, east, south, and west with candles in candle holders on the floor at an equal distance from the center of the circle. If repeatedly kneeling at the candles will be difficult, place them on stools or other raised platforms instead.

Place the small table at the center of the circle to hold the ritual materials, along with the cushion or stool. Leave the ritual space otherwise empty.

On each sheet of paper, write one or more barriers to change. These can be external barriers or internal thoughts and feelings that interfere with change or with the acceptance of change. Each of the four sheets must contain at least one barrier, but the same barrier can be repeated if needed to fill all four sheets.

The Ritual

Using the broom, sweep the floor of the space, moving from the center to the perimeter in each of the four directions. As you sweep, repeat the chant:

> With each brush of the broom, the old gives way to the new.

Kneel or bow your head and light the north candle while you say:

> May the north wind blow change in my life.

Then light the south, east, and west candles, repeating the phrase for wind originating in each direction.

Take the noncombustible bowl and one of the sheets of paper to the north candle. Kneel at the candle, read the barrier aloud, then ignite the paper. Place it in the bowl to burn, reigniting any parts that remain until it is fully consumed.

> May this fire fed by the north wind burn away what is keeping me from change. Repeat with the south, east, and west candles.

Return the ash bowl to the center of the circle and retrieve the bowl of water. Kneel before the north candle, extinguish it, and wave the smoke toward the water. Repeat with the south, east, and west candles.

Return to the center of the circle. Pour enough water from the bowl to thoroughly mix with the ashes in the noncombustible bowl.

> Wind and water of the north, south, east, and west, dissolve all barriers, remove all fears, so that change may enter my life.

Name the change you wish to come.

Take the bowl outdoors and pour the mixture of ashes and water into the ground.

> With this libation of ash and water poured into earth, I plant the seed for change in my life. May change grow in my life. May change flower in my life. May change be the fruit I harvest from this new day on. Ashé.

Enter the new day with determination to be the change.

Variations

This ritual may be performed indoors or outdoors. While this example is written for an individual, it can be adapted for use with a congregation or other community group with a minister or other leader facilitating. The barriers can be written on sheets of paper by members of the congregation, divided into fourths, and burned collectively at each candle. The verbal parts of the ritual can be spoken in unison. The ash and water mixture can be poured into a pot of earth if the ritual is done indoors.

When holding the ritual in a group setting, consider a range of mobility needs. Placing the candles on stools or other raised platforms will avoid the difficulty of repeatedly kneeling to work with objects on the floor.

Questions for Discussion

- What barriers to change are external and what barriers are internal?
- Does the change begin with me or with others?
- Is the change what I wish for?
- Is the change one I must accept and adjust to, though I did not wish it?
- What will be the consequences of this change for me?

Glossary

Adinkra—A system of several dozen visual symbols originating in the culture of the Akan ethnic group of West Africa, each having a philosophical or cultural meaning. The symbols appear in graphic art, fabric designs, and statuary.

Afá—See Ifá.

Afrocentrism—A worldview that centers the history, cultural aesthetics, and perspectives of people of African descent.

Akan—An African ethnic group living primarily in Ghana and the Ivory Coast.

Ashanti—A subgroup of the Akan people (see *Akan*) living in contemporary Ghana and the descendants of a historical kingdom founded in the 1600s.

Ashé—A word originating in the Yoruba culture that refers to a spiritual force that must be in balance for proper existence. Used colloquially, the word expresses solemn or enthusiastic agreement and affirmation. In the African Diaspora, the word may be spoken as a blessing.

Ayao—A female warrior deity in the Yoruba and Santeria religions associated with air.

Azande warriors—A warrior group of the Azande people of central Africa that historically honored same-sex relationships in the precolonial era. The Azande region includes parts of Sudan, the Central African Republic, and the Democratic Republic of Congo.

Baba—"Father" in the Swahili language. The term is used to respectfully address a male elder.

Babalawo—A term literally translated from the Yoruba language as "father of secrets," referring to a priest of the Yoruba religion.

Bakuli la matunda na mboga—Swahili phrase meaning "fruit and vegetable bowl," which is included in the celebration of Kwanzaa (see *Kwanzaa*).

Basaa—A West African ethnic group residing primarily in Liberia.

Bogando—A Ugandan ethnic group, also called the Baganda.

Chi—A life force in the Ibo or Igbo religion that is present in all things to varying degrees.

Chukwu—The Ibo or Igbo name for God.

Dagara—An African ethnic group located in Burkina Faso, Côte d'Ivoire, and Ghana.

Diaspora, African—Term referencing the communities formed by people of African descent who live outside of Africa.

Djembe—A goblet-shaped West African drum traditionally made of wood with a goatskin head that is played by striking various positions on the drumhead with the open hand.

Djun djun—A double-headed cylindrical West African drum traditionally made of wood with goatskin heads at either end that is played with drumsticks. Also called a dunun.

Ewe—A Ghanaian ethnic group.

Fon—An African ethnic group living in Benin, Nigeria, and Togo.

Fulani—A large African ethnic group living throughout western and central Africa.

Harambee—A Swahili word translated as "let's pull together" that is used as an affirmation during Kwanzaa.

Ibo (also Igbo)—A Nigerian ethnic group.

Ifá—A system of divination practiced by the Yoruba people of West Africa.

Imani—A Swahili word translated as "faith." Also one of the seven principles or values celebrated during Kwanzaa.

Juneteenth—An African American holiday recognizing the ending of slavery throughout the United States.

Kalimba (also called mbira dzavadzimu)—An African musical instrument consisting of a wooden sound box with metal tines that produce musical notes when plucked with the thumbs.

Karamu—A Swahili word meaning "supper" or "feast."

Kente—A handwoven fabric made of colorful strips of silk and cotton traditionally worn by royalty in Ghana.

Kikombe cha umoja—A Swahili phrase, translated as "unity cup," referring to the ceremonial cup from which Kwanzaa participants share a communal drink.

Kinara—A candelabrum holding seven candlesticks during Kwanzaa.

King Mwango the Second—A nineteenth-century king of the Baganda People thought to have been openly gay.

Kisii—A Bantu ethnic group in Africa believed to have historically recognized lesbian marriage.

Kiswahili (also called Swahili)—A Bantu language spoken primarily in Kenya, Mozambique, and Tanzania.

Kujichagulia—A Swahili word, translated as "self-determination," referring to one of the seven principles or values celebrated during Kwanzaa.

Kuria—A Bantu ethnic group in Tanzania believed to have historically recognized lesbian marriage.

Kuumba—A Swahili word, translated as "creativity," referring to one of the seven principles or values celebrated during Kwanzaa.

Kwanzaa—An annual African American celebration taking place from December 26 to January 1 that centers on seven principles or values that are intended to build a strong and positive cultural identity.

Luba—An ethnic group living in the Democratic Republic of Congo.

Lubuko—The divination system of the Luba people.

Maafa—A Kiswahili word, translated as "great disaster," referring to the African Transatlantic slave trade.

Mbira dzavadzimu (also called kalimba)—An African musical instrument consisting of a wooden sound box with several rows of metal tines that produce musical notes when plucked with the thumbs and index fingers.

Mendi—An ethnic group living in Sierra Leone.

Mishumaa saba—The seven candles, each representing a principle or value, used during Kwanzaa.

Mkeka—A straw mat symbolizing tradition used during Kwanzaa.

Muhinde—Ears of corn symbolizing children used during Kwanzaa.

Mzungu—A word in the Kinyarwanda language spoken in Rwanda that is used to describe a foreign visitor who is typically White.

Nana—A synonym for grandmother used by African Americans. The term may also be used to respectfully address a female elder in the African Diaspora. In the Akan culture of Ghana, the term may indicate royalty of any gender.

Nandi—A Nilotic-language-speaking ethnic group in Kenya believed to have historically recognized lesbian marriage.

Ndevui—The Mendi people's term for a primal force within nature from which all living existence flows.

Negritude—A 1930s-era intellectual movement of African and African Diaspora writers, poets, and politicians primarily in French-speaking countries that emphasized Black consciousness, antiracism, anticolonialism, and Marxism.

Nguzo Saba—The seven principles or values celebrated during Kwanzaa.

Nia—A Swahili word, translated as "purpose," referring to one of the seven principles or values celebrated during Kwanzaa.

Nilotico Lango—A Nilotic-language-speaking ethnic group in Uganda who are believed to have historically recognized gay marriage.

Nommo—A Bantu language word, translated as "to make one drink" but used contemporaneously to refer to the power of the spoken word.

Ntu—A Bantu term for a primal force within nature from which all living existence flows.

Nuer—A Nilotic-language-speaking ethnic group living in Sudan.

Nzima—An ethnic group living in Ghana thought to have permitted same-sex marriage in precolonial times.

Olokun—A Yoruba deity associated with wealth and oceans.

Oshun—A Yoruba deity associated with rivers.

Oya—A Yoruba deity associated with wind, lightning, and storms.

Queen Nzinga (full name Nzinga Ana de Sousa Mbande)—An African queen during the 1600s who ruled kingdoms in what is now Angola.

Quinceañera—A coming of age celebration in Latin American cultures traditionally occurring on a girl's fifteenth birthday.

Sankofa—A word meaning "to retrieve" in the Twi language spoken in Ghana. Also represented in the Ghanaian Adinkra pictorial system as a bird with its head turned backwards while its feet face forward to convey the importance of history and wisdom from the past.

Santeria (also known as Regla de Ocha and Regla Lucumi)—An African Diasporic religion developed in Cuba that combines elements of the Yoruba and Roman Catholic religions.

Shango—A Yoruba deity associated with thunder and lightning.

Ubuntu—An African philosophical concept that emphasizes human interdependence.

Ujamaa—A Swahili word, translated as "cooperative economics," referring to one of the seven principles or values celebrated during Kwanzaa.

Ujima—A Swahili word, translated as "collective work and responsibility," referring to one of the seven principles or values celebrated during Kwanzaa.

Umoja—A Swahili word, translated as "unity," referring to one of the seven principles or values celebrated during Kwanzaa.

Umoja Karamu—A Swahili phrase translated as "unity feast."

Yemaya—A Yoruba deity associated with bodies of water.

Yewa—A Yoruba deity associated with water, virginity, and death.

Yoruba—The religion of the Yoruba people, originating in Nigeria, characterized by an intricate cosmology, highly developed rituals and philosophical traditions, and an elaborate system of divination.